TWO NOVELS OF MEXICO

"These two short novels are among Azuela's best; they are full of humor and pathos, and written in a racy popular style. Professor Simpson's version is superb. He has been able to keep in the translation the freshness, color, and intensity of the original."—Arturo Torres-Rioseco.

Two
Novels of
Mexico

The Flies
The Bosses

BY MARIANO AZUELA
Translated from the Spanish
BY LESLEY BYRD SIMPSON

UNIVERSITY OF CALIFORNIA PRESS
Berkeley, Los Angeles, London

UNIVERSITY OF CALIFORNIA PRESS
Berkeley and Los Angeles, California

UNIVERSITY OF CALIFORNIA PRESS, LTD.
London, England

First English Edition

ISBN: 0-520-00053-6

*Originally published in Spanish as
Los Caciques,* Mexico, Compañía Periodística
Nacional, 1917; 2d ed., Mexico, Ed. de "La
Razón," 1931. *Las Moscas y Domitilo quiere
ser Diputado,* Mexico, Tip. de Carranza e
hijos, 1918; 2d ed., Mexico, Ed. de "La
Razón," 1931.

Printed in the United States of America

9 0

PREFACE

Forty-five short years ago, while the Western world was still dozing in the twilight of the nineteenth century, the Mexican Revolution exploded. It was at first accepted as just another Latin election in the Richard Harding Davis tradition, not to be taken seriously. We had long since got used to the comfortable notion that Mexico, in the deep quietness of the dictatorship of Don Porfirio Díaz, was safe and sound. The peso was at par; that elderly magician, Don José Limantour, Don Porfirio's Minister of the Treasury, had made Mexico respectable in the financial centers of Europe and America; Don Porfirio himself, at eighty-odd, still seemed to have a lot of life left in his weathered frame. The rigged election of 1910 had come off according to plan and Don Porfirio was again President. But somehow things began to go wrong. A dreamy little man named Francisco Madero had published a not very exciting book entitled *The Presidential Succession of 1910* and had followed it up (while doing a short stretch in the jail of San Luis Potosí) with a political manifesto known as "The Plan of San Luis Potosí." In the first he suggested the awesome possibility that Don Porfirio might not live forever; in the second he demanded free elections. Several obstreperous characters, namely, Francisco Villa and Pascual Orozco of Chihuahua, and Emiliano Zapata of Morelos, took advantage of the occasion to stage a revolution, which unexpectedly caught on, and in a very short time the whole country was in flames and Don Porfirio's parade army of *federales* was on the run before a wild mob of fighting peasants and cowboys. Don Porfirio was forced to fly the country, and in the free election of 1911 the unknown Madero, now a popular hero, was the overwhelming choice of the voters.

Madero believed in brotherly love and sweetness and light. He trusted his enemies. Fifteen months later, a well-organized counterrevolution, headed by his own General Victoriano Huerta, seized the government. President Madero and Vice-President Pino Suárez were shot "while attempting to escape," which touched off a many-pronged civil war, as the various leaders of the Revolution sought to eliminate each other. For five years it dragged out its sanguinary course. Pancho Villa dominated the Aguascalientes Convention of October, 1914, and he and the formidable Emiliano Zapata enjoyed that winter a brief but lurid occupation of Mexico City. But the barbarous conduct of Villa and his troops in the capital outraged the nation. General Alvaro Obregón deserted him and "pronounced" for the "First Chief of the Revolution," Governor Carranza of Coahuila. Striking swiftly from Vera Cruz, Obregón defeated Zapata at Puebla and chased the Villa and Zapata forces out of Mexico City. Then at Celaya, Guanajuato, he whipped Villa in three days of the bloodiest fighting of the war. Zapata, disillusioned with Villa, went back to his private war in the south. After the disaster at Celaya, Villa entrained his army at Irapuato and fled to Agua Prieta, Sonora, where he was cornered and definitely crushed in the summer of 1915 by Obregón and Plutarco Elías Calles.

Such, in brief, is the background of these two remarkable vignettes of the Revolution, drawn from life by the late Dr. Mariano Azuela (1873–1952). At the time of his death Azuela was the grand old man of Mexican letters. His life spanned the stormy years of the dissolution of the Old Régime and the Revolution. He was one of the many thoughtful men who had rebelled against the stifling and interminable dictatorship of Porfirio Díaz and who looked to Francisco Madero as the prophet of a new Mexico, a Mexico of freedom and democracy. Azuela served in the medical corps of Villa's army until Villa's defeat, after which he took refuge in El Paso and had nothing further to do with Mexican politics. His post gave him an incomparable opportunity to observe the actions and antics of a frightened people, and he set down his impressions in a series of poignant and frequently hilarious sketches, and one full-length novel, *The Underdogs* (*Los de Abajo*, 1916).

The sketches, notably *The Bosses* (*Los Caciques*, 1917) and *The Flies* (*Las Moscas*, 1918), have been undeservedly neglected, probably because of the impact of *The Underdogs*. They are, nevertheless, very much worth reading, being, so to speak, pages from a journal written hotly from life. Of *The Flies* my distinguished friend, Arturo Torres-Ríoseco, writes: "In *The Flies* Azuela's humor achieves its full expression. . . . Instead of giving us descriptions of battles, he contents himself with showing the effects of the Revolution upon the cowards and the shameless opportunists. Poltroons and drunkards, caught up in the mortal terror of flight, see on every hand the pistols of Carranza's troops, or they see themselves cowering before the brutal *dorados* of Pancho Villa—people without ideals, bargain-counter revolutionaries, once servants of Díaz, then of Madero, later of Huerta, and finally of Villa. Tomorrow they will join up with Carranza, Obregón, Calles. No matter. The important thing is to live, dress well, eat, enjoy life." (Arturo Torres-Ríoseco, *Novelistas contemporáneos de América,* Santiago, Chile, 1939, p. 40.)

The action of *The Flies* opens during a panic in a railway station of Mexico City. Politicians, government clerks, generals and officers of the old federal army (the cynical "ex-federals" of the story), doctors, teachers, women of easy virtue, and ladies of shaky respectability, all those, in brief, who had short-sightedly thrown in with Villa, are striving desperately to escape their imagined death at the hands of Obregón's Yaqui Indian troops, who enjoyed a well-earned reputation for ferocity. The frightened refugees crowd into a hospital car, where throughout the night we listen to their wild surmises.

Azuela's style in this story, staccato or even telegraphic, is admirably suited to suggest the jerky movement of the train, the nervousness of the fugitives, their naked fear. The choppy, fragmentary dialogue, the abrupt shifts, the callousness of some, the maudlin drunkenness of others, and the prodigious silliness of the frightened mother and her gold-digging family, together give us an etching of civil war not easily forgotten.

The somber tone of *The Bosses* is as remote as possible from the raucous gaiety of *The Flies.* The story is laid two years earlier, during the brief administration of the luckless Madero and the grim reaction of the sinister Huerta. The action takes place in a small western city which is dominated and virtually owned by a merchant-banker-landlord family of parasites, the Del Llanos (the *caciques,* or bosses), who had risen to power and affluence under Porfirio Díaz and who now boggle at no measure, however low or violent, to maintain their privileges.

Azuela, who had served as mayor of Lagos de Moreno (Jalisco) under Madero, knew and shared the bitterness of the victims of *caciquismo* (bossism), and makes no attempt to hide it. It is difficult for us at this distance to accept the monstrosities of the Del Llano family—the cynical priest, Father Jeremiah, and the cold-blooded Don Ignacio; but Azuela is writing in white-hot anger against the cruelty and injustice of a system and uses the effective device of extreme caricature to point up his thesis, much as José Clemente Orozco pilloried the Mexican middle class in his frescoes later on. Azuela's scalding humor boils over most of all on the jackals and stool pigeons in the pay of the caciques.

The rest of the cast is treated gently. The grocer, Juan Viñas, a kind of Mexican Poor Richard, his saintly wife, Elena, and his two children, Esperanza and Juanito, victims of the system, are necessarily the opposites of the caciques. The author here runs the risk of oversimplification, of drawing a naive black-and-white picture, but he accepts the risk and through his art makes his picture plausible. He does so by employing the same technique that was so successful in *The Flies,* by allowing his characters to portray themselves with all their human failings. He engages our sympathy even for the fatuous, childish, and pigheaded grocer, whose unintelligent loyalty to the caciques brings destruction down on himself and his family. Azuela is equally tender with Don Timoteo, the fuzzy-minded freethinker, who is baffled by the secondhand socialism he reads in his radical sheet. The meetings of the revolutionary Twentieth of November Club are as innocent as Don Timoteo himself and are reported with the same understanding deftness that makes the dialogue in the hospital car of *The Flies* alive and convincing.

The burden of the narrative is carried by Rodríguez, the lonely poet and intellectual, and the only clear head among the small town radicals. He is the noblest of Azuela's creations. Half mad as he is, Rodríguez is a wonderfully attractive personality, with his despair over the human race and his pity for stray dogs and cats and all helpless creatures. The love story of Rodríguez and Esperanza Viñas is heartbreaking in its intensity. Rodríguez sees the inevitable catastrophe in store for himself and those he loves and can do nothing to avert it, but goes to his brutal death defying his murderers, very much like the heroic Belisario Domínguez, who faced certain assassination for denouncing the ineffable Huerta in the Mexican Congress.

The story builds up to an apocalyptic climax. Popular revulsion at the murder of President Madero brings the Revolution to the Del Llanos' city. In the shooting and confusion, Juan Viñas' young son Juanito suddenly grows up and sees with deadly clarity the cause of his and his sister's tragedy. With her help he sets fire to the new building of Del Llano Bros., Inc., the hated symbol of their misfortunes, and "entranced, hand in hand, they watched the flames mount to the purple sky."

If the reader is shocked by such melodrama, he is reminded that those fearful years of the civil war were full of such episodes. What may seem overdrawn to us was commonplace in revolutionary Mexico, and if Azuela describes the time in sharp focus, with naturalistic violence, it is not only justifiable; it is right.

It was in 1931. I don't know what I expected, but I was a little nervous about meeting the great satirist. I was certainly not prepared for the gentle and dignified neighborhood doctor who met me at the door of his old-fashioned, somewhat shabby, but comfortable house in a poor quarter of Mexico City, near the Estación Colonia. He greeted me with a cordial *abrazo*. He was a stoutish man in his late fifties, his lively eyes twinkling behind thick glasses. He looked, indeed, very much like one of the respectable people who take such a drubbing in his stories. Half a dozen patients, evidently penniless, were stoically waiting in a stuffy reception room, notwithstanding which Don Mariano pulled me into his office and offered me a chair and a cigarette. He was dying to talk. His patients could wait.

I began by asking him why he, the most famous Mexican writer of his day, was still practicing medicine instead of devoting himself to literature. "After all," I said, "there must be hundreds of able and willing young physicians to look after your patients, but there is only one Mariano Azuela to write the classics of the Revolution. Surely . . ."

"My friend," he interrupted, peering at me quizzically, a glance half-pitying, half-deprecating, "my friend, do you know how many copies of my books are sold here in Mexico? Naturally, you don't. Well, if the sale of any one of them should reach a thousand it would be a sensation. No. We Mexicans don't support our writers. Some day, possibly, but not now. Just take a look at the book stalls and what do you find? A lot of bad translations of second-rate French novels and the like. So I practice medicine and write when I can find the time."

I suggested that I should like to put some of his sketches of the Revolution into English, whereupon he gave me a lecture on the art of translating. "The translator," he said, as I recall his words, "has a two-way duty: to the author and to the public for whom he is translating. The translator must, somehow, see into the author's thought, beyond the words, and he must make it intelligible. Figures of speech in one language may have no counterpart in the other. The setting, the manners, a whole way of life, must be re-created in the new medium. I won't say it can't be done, but it is difficult."

He was right, of course. I set to work and soon found myself stumped. During the year I laid a good many problems in Don Mariano's lap and found him invariably patient, understanding, and discouraging. He plainly thought I was wasting my time. But there was something insistently nagging about the task. Over the years my pile of discarded versions grew. At the same time my knowledge of Mexico grew, until today I think I am not too far from Don Mariano's "thought beyond the words."

Don Mariano was a kind of saint, a beloved lay saint, sometimes a skeptical and severe saint, but full of charity for his people, whose weaknesses he saw, as he saw his own, clear-eyed and unflinching. I suspect that the disillusioned Doctor of *The Flies* and the tortured Rodríguez of *The Bosses,* together form a self-portrait. I offer this translation as a tribute to the memory of a great man.

Lesley Byrd Simpson

THE FLIES

CONTENTS

I	THE PANIC	5
II	LONG LIVE THE GOVERNOR!	14
III	NIGHT-BIRDS	19
IV	REBIRTH	26
V	VICTIM OF THE REVOLUTION	33
VI	THE GENERAL	37
VII	VADE RETRO	42
VIII	MR. SECRETARY!	52
IX	UNWELCOME ENCOUNTER	56
X	RESPECTABLE PEOPLE	63
XI	EXPONENT OF ENERGY	68
XII	VILLA PAPER	76
XIII	A MOTHER'S HEROISM	83
XIV	CURTAIN	86

LIST OF CHARACTERS

TIME: April, 1915.

THE REYES-TÉLLEZ FAMILY, *consisting of:*
> MARTA, *the mother;*
> MATILDE, *the elder daughter;*
> ROSITA, *the younger daughter;*
> RUBÉN, *the son.*

QUIÑONES, *a schoolmate of Rubén.*

DONACIANO RÍOS, *a prosecuting attorney.*

RODOLFO BOCANEGRA, *a politician.*

NEFTALÍ SANCHO PEREDO DE LA GARZA, *a poet.*

DON SINFOROSO, *mayor of Turicato, in the uniform of a colonel of the federal army.*

A TAILOR AND A NOTARY, *as majors in the same.*

SEÑOR RUBALCABA, *a schoolmaster.*
> RAQUEL AND AURORA, *teachers in his school.*

GENERAL MALACARA.
> CACHUCHA AND MANUELA, *his protégées.*
> BERMÚDEZ, *his orderly.*

MORALITOS, *a government clerk.*

THE DOCTOR.
> NICOMEDES, *his orderly.*

THE MAJOR.

VARIOUS EX-FEDERAL OFFICERS.

THE DORADOS, *troops of Villa's bodyguard.*

FRANCISCO VILLA (*Doroteo Arango*) *General of the Northern Division of the Revolutionary Army.*

I THE PANIC

Drums crashed and bugles blew. The crowd divided and made a lane for the soldiers. Matilde elbowed her way through the ranks, indifferent to the laughter of the bystanders.

"Mama, my canary! Rubén! Rosita! This way!"

Marta trotted after her, puffing, lugging a heavy valise and the bird cage. The two went on as far as a string of box cars that blocked their way. The soldiers broke ranks and swarmed to the roofs of the cars. Marta, out of breath and exhausted, dropped the valise.

"Where are Rubén and Rosita?" she asked in pantomime.

"Rosita is smart, Mama. She'll find us."

Matilde put her lips to the cage.

"Darling! Lover! Give me a kiss!"

The little creature was beating its wings nervously against the bars.

"Matilde, there's Señor Ríos! Perhaps he can tell us. Señor Ríos! Señor Ríos!"

A tragic head, mounted on a skinny neck, emerged from the moving sea of faces. Señor Ríos made his way to Marta and Matilde and greeted them with great courtesy.

"So Rubén and Rosita are lost, are they? Well, they're not the only ones. We're all lost!"

His heavy eyebrows, like two hairy black caterpillars, reared and met. He approached Matilde.

"Querétaro has fallen!"

But the two women were not interested in Querétaro and asked again about Rubén and Rosita. Señor Ríos scowled in a tremendous effort to concentrate. All the lines of his face deepened. He wrinkled up his nose and blew it twice.

"Yes, the Carranzistas are within ten miles of the capital. We're lost, hopelessly lost!"

"Oh dear, where are my children?" cried Marta, casting anxious glances in all directions.

"Señor Ríos says we're lost!" mumbled the bystanders.

The rumor flew, leaving pale faces and fallen jaws in its wake. Señor Ríos hitched up his perpetually bagging trousers, blew his nose twice again and made his escape.

"I must see the governor at once!"

Marta wrung her hands.

"What shall we do?"

"Were you asking about Rubén and Rosita? I saw them just now with a soldier at the end of that train."

"Oh yes, with General Malacara! Oh Moralitos, how good you are! We're so grateful! Come, Mama, give me the canary and you bring the valise. Come!"

"If I didn't have to see the governor immediately I'd be only too glad to go with you," said Moralitos in a hollow voice, showing the whites of his eyes.

"We're lost!" he said to Marta tragically.

Marta and Matilde followed the track as far as the siding, where trains were standing end to end. There they halted and Matilde raised the cage to her eyes.

"Darling! Angel! Give me a kiss!"

But the canary, bedraggled and exhausted, huddled

behind the seed cup. He fixed his beady little eyes on Matilde, but refused her painted lips.

After a moment's indecision Marta and Matilde crossed the track into the huge switch yard inside a wooden fence. The tangled skein of rails gleamed through the pickets. Numerous trains, bursting with people, stood near the office and freight sheds of the station. Whistles blew endlessly, bellowing like wounded bulls, or shrieking like maniacs.

Marta's face, framed in a shawl knotted about her stringy neck, was beaded with perspiration. She dropped the valise.

"Well, what do we do now, Matilde? My ears are ringing and my head's spinning."

She sat down heavily on the valise and her tired gaze lost itself in the heaving crowd. Even Matilde, now red as a poppy, was beginning to waver.

"Mama! Matilde! Here we are!"

Marta and Matilde looked in the direction of the distant shout, vainly.

"Matilde! Here in the hospital car!"

"I see them, Mama! Come! Bring the valise. There's Rosita looking out the door!"

But it was not easy to penetrate the hospital car. A man in khaki and a wide hat blocked the door and looked at them sourly.

"Doctor, these are my mother and my sister Matilde," explained Rosita.

"This is not a passenger coach, young lady."

"But there isn't room for a pin in the other cars, doctor. Just look!"

Rosita insisted, but the doctor was silent.

"Come down at once, Rosita! Come down, Rubén!"

said Matilde haughtily. "General Malacara will find us a place."

"But he's the very one who brought us here," said Rubén.

"All right," growled the doctor. "Climb on."

Whereupon he retreated to the far end of the car among the gleaming fittings of his field cot and the bottles of his shop.

"Did you really see the general, Matilde?" whispered Rubén.

"Of course not!" answered Matilde, smiling. "I just use him for our magic wand."

"Damned sawbones!" raged Rubén, beating the floor with his bamboo cane.

A long and timid silence followed. Only Rosita took things calmly. She looked out the door. Her fresh face and neat turnout made a pleasing contrast with the surrounding neglect and slovenliness. The morning was glorious under a spotless sky. The warm spring greenness extended beyond the white patios and spread over the immense valley dotted with splashes of red tile. Rosita was happy. She hummed "Mari-Mari" in her sweet clear voice.

Below them the multitude buzzed like an overturned beehive, pullulated like a swarm of silkworms, spilling over the dusty yard, piling up in the cars, on the roofs, on the platforms, showing their grimy heads above the sides of coal cars, clinging to oil and water tanks.

Marta counted her children over and over again. She sighed with relief.

"One, two, three! Yes, thank God, they're all here!"

Marta was tireless in her thanks, but her joy was

suddenly dampened as she remembered Moralitos' tragic look and the despair of Señor Ríos. She called her children to her.

"Nonsense, Mama!" said Rubén. "Señor Ríos is just chicken-hearted."

"But Moralitos said. . . ."

"Moralitos likes to let on he knows it all."

"General Malacara assured me," said Rosita seriously, "that he will deliver us at our own house safe and sound inside of a week."

"It's a week's vacation for us and sure promotion for our loyalty to the cause," affirmed Rubén with a swagger, toying with his stick.

Marta refused to share the general optimism.

"My heart tells me we're in danger, children. Rubén, the doctor must know how things are. Go ask him."

"Me? Speak to that baboon?"

"You, then, Matilde."

Matilde drew up her arrogant bust proudly.

Rosita looked toward the end of the car where the doctor was pasting labels on bottles. She approached him slowly. Her step was smooth and rhythmical. Her slender figure swayed. Her tight skirt did justice to her thighs.

"Doctor, we aren't in any danger, are we?"

The doctor raised his head and looked sharply at Rosita. He finished labelling a bottle and made his way to the group.

"Would you mind telling me who the devil put it into your heads that we're all running away?"

He looked out astonished at the general panic in the station. Not an empty space was to be seen. Many would have been glad to find a foothold on an iron step. The crowd of civilians was so dense that the dead color of dirty khaki was lost in the flowing black of broadcloth. The presence of troops could only be guessed at by the occasional gleam of a rifle barrel above the formless mass of heads.

The most recent arrivals were milling about like frightened ants. Too scared to return to their homes, they took off up the roads and trails leading to the hamlets, villages, and ravines of the mountains.

Rosita was about to answer the doctor's question when Matilde stopped her emphatically.

"It's plain to be seen that the doctor doesn't live here! Here in the capital we know pretty well why we are frightened when we hear 'The Carranzistas are coming!' We know what those Yaqui devils are capable of! Did you hear, doctor, what the Carranzistas said when some of our best people congratulated them for beating the federals? I hate them so much I can't speak calmly! Well, don't look for the answer in the cemeteries, because the dead can't talk! Why, they turned our most distinguished houses into barracks and our schools into taverns! They stabled their horses in the archbishop's palace and used our churches for pigsties!"

"And, doctor," added Marta in tears, "they even used the holy cathedral for a maternity hospital!"

"Which shows that the troops have made undeniable progress in the field of hygiene," observed an individual who had just climbed on board. He wore a major's star on his hat. His eyes were lively, his beard was white, and his lips had an ironic twist.

"And I suppose," retorted Matilde furiously, "I

suppose that the graves of the bishops and archbishops in the cathedral were also violated for purposes of hygiene!"

"Ah well," put in Rubén, who always tried to divine what the officers were thinking, ready to chime in with them on all occasions, "they do say that revolution is revolution."

Rosita was not interested and went to the door of the car humming a dance tune. Her white throat and full breasts vibrated gently to the music.

"Are you in the government service?" asked the major, drawing up a bench and offering them a seat.

"We were born in the service, so to speak," answered Marta. "My husband was doorkeeper of the National Palace from the time of the Emperor Maximilian down to Don Panchito Madero. He kept his job there until he died."

Marta broke off as her voice drowned in a sudden flood of tears.

"We come from a poor but respectable family," added Matilde.

"Do you know that we belong to the Reyes-Téllez of Culiacán?" asked Marta, unexpectedly serene as a spring sky.

"When I was in the fifth grade," said Matilde, half closing her eyes in reminiscence, "I went to work in the Public Library. And Rosita was still in short dresses when she got a job as a stenographer in the State Department. Rubén works at the Normal School. . . . Darling! Angel! You little beauty! You spoiled baby!"

The canary was hopping about its cage chirping. It put its beak to Matilde's offered lips.

Marta told the sad story of the sack of the cathedral. Oh, the mountains of cassocks, surplices, stoles, capes, and ornaments, heaped up on the broken chairs, empty shelves, and on the floor! And oh, the embroidered cloth all ripped to shreds as savage fingers tore at the gold braid strand by strand!

Rosita was leaning against the crossbar of the door. Matilde saw that something was wrong and went up to her. Rosita, scowling, was staring fixedly at a point in the crowd. Matilde followed her gaze.

"It does look like a general," she said to herself.

The general's back was turned, but the broad shoulders, the square head, the slow movements, and the gray hair showing under the rim of his hat, left no room for doubt.

"Is it he?" she whispered in Rosita's ear.

"Of course! Who else could be so shameless?"

Matilde noticed two young women who were laughing familiarly with the general. Their rude manners and tasteless finery proclaimed to the world that they were untamed girls brought in by the soldiers from the mountains of Durango or Chihuahua. Matilde smiled and patted Rosita's angry cheek.

"How much did Father Espinosa say the sacred vessels of the cathedral were worth?" asked Marta.

"Why, one of the chalices alone was worth a fortune! It was solid gold inlaid with precious stones."

"Gold! *Voilà l'ennemi!*" mumbled the major half to himself.

Rubén thought he could guess what was in the major's mind.

"The Carranzista flag," he said, "bears the motto *Death and Extermination to the Reaction!* Well, since

to the Carranzistas gold and the reaction are synony-
mous. . . ."

"They can't stand the gold up against a wall," cut
in Matilde, "and that's why they have to be satisfied
with stealing it. And yet they do well enough. They
put an end to the Reaction by putting it into their
pockets!"

"Well, as your brother just said, revolution is revolution."

"Yes, major, but revolution is one thing and banditry is quite another. You, for example, are revolutionaries, not bandits."

"How do you figure that out?" asked the doctor
contemptuously.

"Very easily. You can recognize decent people from
a distance."

Marta and Matilde outdid each other in praise of
the doctor and the major, much to the astonishment
of the two officers.

"Thinkers prepare the revolution," muttered the
major absently; "bandits carry it out. At the moment
no one can say with assurance: 'So-and-so is a revolutionary and What's-his-name is a bandit.' Tomorrow,
perhaps, it will be easier."

"Nonsense!" interrupted the doctor. "It's a problem
in elementary arithmetic. Let us suppose that we wish
to discover the equivalent value x of a certain hero
named So-and-so. Let us further suppose that before
the revolution x equalled zero pesos. But, since So-
and-so couldn't have acquired a single peso without
stealing it, by cancellation we derive the result: x
equals a bandit!"

"Q. E. D.," added Rubén, as the doctor's sally was
greeted with a burst of laughter.

II LONG LIVE THE GOVERNOR!

The crowd stirred with excitement. A locomotive gave two toots. A bell rang, couplings crashed, and a train backed in under the shed, plowing its way through the sea of anxious heads, and disappeared like a playing card in a deck among the infinity of cars that covered every foot of track: cars stuffed with people, broken cars, cars patched with great expanses of white boards newly planed, engines with new plates of shining steel. Safety valves hissed deafeningly.

Matilde, erect and arrogant, approached Rosita.

"Well, what happened to your general?"

Rosita poured out a flood of abuse, but her eyes belied her.

"That's the way it always is," remarked Matilde. "You think you're raising someone from the gutter, when all you're doing is lowering yourself to his level."

She bit her lip thoughtfully, while Rosita's sharp heels beat a tattoo on the floor.

"Are you sure he saw you?"

"What difference does that make?"

"Well, if he didn't see you he didn't insult you."

Rosita stared at her sister uncomprehendingly.

"Think it over and don't lose your head."

"I don't see how you can make excuses for him."

"Tell me this, Rosita: did he see you, or didn't he?"

"To tell the truth, I really don't know. They were coming straight toward the car and I got so mad I turned my back. When I looked again they were gone."

"And of course that means the conduct of the general was not that of a perfect gentleman! Do have a little sense, child! Don't you see he did notice you and turned away to keep from embarrassing you? What more do you want?"

"But does that excuse his flaunting those . . . those women in front of everyone?"

"But, Rosita, he's a *general.*"

Matilde brandished her logic so effectively that she finally succeeded in clearing the general's name.

A bugle corps in the distance was playing the march of honor. The applause was drowned by shouting.

"The governor! The governor!"

The crowd made a lane.

A tightly packed mass of civilians, leavened by a few soldiers, blackened the horizon. The silhouettes of bent shoulders, craning necks, and adoring faces surrounded a vigorous head, whose thick, beardless lips wore a smile of supreme indolence.

Matilde felt herself inspired. The universal enthusiasm exploded in a burst of hand clapping as the escort passed. Matilde waited at the door of the hospital car until the governor was opposite her.

"Governor," she cried in ringing tones, "you are the very image of our Father Cuauhtémoc! You have the soul of the noble Aztec race! Long live Mexico! Long live the governor!"

The courtiers stared in amazed admiration.

"Bravo! Admirable! Well said! Exactly so! Bravo! Magnificent!"

Anxious necks stretched in anticipation of the governor's beneficent glance, but his colorless smile hardly changed. He raised his head.

"Who is that girl?"

One of the late arrivals noticed that the hospital car was empty and, before the doctor could protest, the mob had scrambled on board and filled it to overflowing. The doctor folded his arms in a fury and ground his teeth. The major grinned mockingly.

Government clerks recognized each other, saluted and embraced. Moralitos, a short, fat, spindle-shanked, grotesque sort of monkey-on-a-stick, looked for a place in which to deposit a little old woman who he said was his grandmother. Having got her settled, he opened his eyes enormously and eagerly sought out Matilde. In his haste to reach her side he stepped on everybody.

"Matilde, you were wonderful! I congratulate you from my heart! Wonderful! Sublime!"

He congratulated the rest of the family. He couldn't stop.

"What an intelligence! What a head! Isn't it true, gentlemen, that Matilde made a hit?"

Moralitos turned to receive the expected applause; but the doctor, like a fiddle string stretched too tightly, exploded.

"It's all very well for you to praise the young lady! That's *your* business."

Moralitos, taken by surprise, wrinkled his mask-like face in astonishment.

"What is not so well," went on the doctor, "is the governor's approval of you. A revolutionary like him? Why, when he smiled at you, you practically committed treason!"

The clerks exchanged nudges.

"Bah! The incense that these vermin burn, major, is full of poison!"

"But, doctor," protested Moralitos, "we are sincere! We are loyal to the government and we are here precisely to prove our devotion to the cause, even if we die for it!"

The doctor glanced at him and turned his back.

"It isn't their fault," he said to the major. "They are only what they have to be. Things go all right with them when everything is subordinated to the most imperious of their bodily needs. They are tormented by it. You understand, major?"

He pressed his stomach languidly.

"Their ideas, their opinions, their sentiments— everything is inspired by their bellies. That's why we can't blame them. But the painful and deplorable part of the business is that we have spilled so much blood only to fall in the end into the clutches of such scum!"

Moralitos showed the whites of his eyes and shivered.

"How's that for discipline, Señor Ríos! Did you hear what he said about the governor?"

The horrified listeners mumbled something about

the doctor's having insulted the first magistrate of the state, but no one dared protest except by grunts and head-waggings.

The engine gave two long and threatening growls. The crowd stirred. Passengers put their heads out the windows and looked for their friends. Handkerchiefs fluttered. Hands—white, brown, fine, or coarse—were raised in salute. Some were grasped. Mournful faces and reddened eyes peered out.

Moralitos, magnificent in black alpaca and white duck, took his stand at the door of the car as if he were the only passenger. He felt himself something of a hero.

The first military train, the governor's, was rudely bumped and had begun to roll when General Malacara and his two gaudy females rushed up and demanded places in the hospital car.

Matilde and Rosita exchanged perplexed glances. Matilde froze. Rosita turned a bright scarlet. But Rubén went to the general's assistance, offered his hands to the girls and helped them on board in a brotherly fashion.

"Thank you! Thank you! Good lad! Courteous as ever!" said the general, giving Rubén a protective pat on the shoulder.

III NIGHT-BIRDS

Songs ended in hoarse shouts and insane laughter. Drunken officers and students made merry with the general's girls, who were somewhat the worse for wear and were lurching about squealing. Toward midnight they began to give out. Their speech became incoherent and inarticulate and then degenerated into howls, hiccoughs, and the weak whimpers that herald the approach of insensibility. They lay, legs outspread, in a heap of bodies overcome by fatigue and alcohol. Nothing now broke the silence but the tired panting of the engine as the train wound its way swiftly through the countryside. The steel of the rails reflected the sky which could be glimpsed occasionally through the patches of prickly pear in the uncertain light of the stars. A stream of sparks splashed in the darkness and started little fires here and there in the dry grass.

Señor Ríos could not close his eyes because he had a conviction that they were about to be attacked. His gaze was fixed on the dark valley. A sudden panic took him by the throat. He thought he saw suspicious shapes along the right of way. Good God! The Carranzistas! He tried to scream, but his voice failed him. What was the use, anyway? The soldiers were all dead drunk. Finally, plucking courage from his very agony, he asked himself whether he might not be the victim of an illusion. He had not eaten for twenty-eight hours. And then he had such a nervous temperament! He rubbed his eyes and explored the landscape more attentively. And behold! a vague shadow rose abruptly from the ground, grew in an instant to gigantic size, and quickly took itself off and disappeared. And then another, and another, and another!

Crack, crack, crack! Shots? A cold sweat trickled from his neck to the base of his spine. He distinctly heard the impact of a bullet against the side of the car. Crack, crack, crack! Christ! A whole regiment was firing at them! His legs were trembling so violently that he had to support himself. The red flame of a grass fire brought him back to life. The suspicious figures resolved themselves into telegraph poles, and he decided that the explosions were caused by the heels of the multitude riding on the roof of the car. The procession of thin shadows was so rhythmical, so monotonous and interminable that a feeling of peace crept into him, and his eyes as dry as blotting paper began to close.

Señor Ríos could not convince himself that he in person could really be traveling so far from his warm fireside. Through his half closed eyes he saw the white and luminous streets of his native town, his little house in the suburbs, sharp and distinct, its garden, its many trees, its birds, and its quietness. He entered. There was the clear blue fountain where the little fishes zigzagged like tongues of flame above the clean sand. His study door was open. The eucalyptus-scented air blew gustily through the great window that looked out on the wood near by.

Señor Ríos nodded, his neck gave way, and he fell insensible on the knees of his neighbor. He felt again the delight of a soft mattress and fresh linen sheets. He dreamed that his escape from the capital on a cattle train was only a dreadful nightmare.

The vertiginous pounding of the wheels echoed in the silence of the countryside. The track was clear. Red signals flashed by, and switchmen's cabins, and the whitewashed walls and iron roofs of the stations. At long intervals the train stopped at some important place. Muffled and silent figures bestirred themselves, boarded the train, and trampled the sleeping passengers.

Señor Ríos awoke with a start, his eyes wild and his hands pressing his heart to keep it from jumping out of his mouth. An attack! Almighty God! He stared about him in terror. The martial notes of a bugle were sounding in his ears.

A long shadowy figure sat opposite him. A pale ascetic face smiled at him sweetly, with ineffable gentleness—a wide, serene face, the eyes lighted by infinite goodness. Señor Ríos felt a kind of ecstasy.

"Are you our blessed Father St. Francis?" he would have liked to ask, but his natural timidity and the iron discipline of the government clerk kept him within the bounds of discretion.

"It's that gentleman snoring," explained the apparition in an unctuous voice. "I couldn't sleep either."

His long white hand indicated General Malacara, who was lying on his back between his women. The general's neck was expanding and contracting like an accordion and he sounded like a whole pigsty. His dream explained, Señor Ríos thanked the friendly shadow with a melancholy smile.

The kerosene lamp that swung from the roof and feebly illuminated the recesses of the car, blinked and went out. Spiritual communication between Señor Ríos and the stranger was soon established, a current of mutual sympathy. Dispensing with preliminaries, Señor Ríos heaved a desolate sigh and exclaimed:

"It's all up with us, don't you think?"

"So it seems," affirmed the apparition in honeyed tones.

Señor Ríos sobbed hopelessly.

"It isn't as bad as all that, Señor Ríos," murmured a familiar voice.

"Ah, Moralitos, you too?"

"Incidents of war, of no real significance," added another voice from a distance.

Seeing that many who seemed to be soundly sleeping were as wide awake as he, Señor Ríos was comforted.

A new silence, interrupted only by the chorus of snorers that served to demonstrate the supremacy of the general's lungs. An occasional deep and painful sigh escaped from the lips of Señor Ríos.

"Have you any children, Señor Ríos?"

With a feeling that he was dictating his will, Señor Ríos answered: "Donaciano Ríos, forty years old; married; two children; government clerk since I cut my eye teeth. Record? Spotless, from the moment I began as a junior clerk in a justice's office until I took my present job as prosecuting attorney. Work? Like a typewriter. With a little cleaning and overhauling and a bit of oil now and then it will run forever and give satisfaction. Outstanding qualities? Utter abdication of will, unlimited moral flexibility, complete lack of individuality. In short, an ideal public servant."

The apparition was enchanted with his new friend and by their astonishing affinity of desires, thoughts, feelings.

"Am I by chance," he asked, "addressing the former Justice of the Supreme Court of Erongarícuaro who served during the memorable days of Our Great President? So? Well, I am Rodolfo Bocanegro, one time state's attorney for Chamácuaro and at present financial director of the state."

"Ah!" cried Señor Ríos, opening his arms and seeking his friend in the darkness. "You were state's attorney in the time of our General Huerta? Very happy to make your acquaintance! What a delightful surprise!"

They shook hands effusively and opened their hearts wide.

"It's hard to believe, isn't it?"

"True."

"They have ruined us!"

"Just about."

'It's anarchy, that's what it is!"

'Exactly."

"We're at the mercy of a lot of bandits!"

As their meaning mounted, their voices subsided, until they were as unsubstantial as a breath and hardly more perceptible.

"To think we suffered the torture of passing from a great government to the tragic farce of Madero, and then from another strong and honest government to this savagery!"

"And yet, Señor Ríos, we have learned something from it. Have you never considered the stoicism we have learned from our long hours of travail? Has it never occurred to you that our serenity reveals that we are guided by something superior to ourselves?"

Señor Ríos frankly confessed that he had seen no evidence of that superior something.

"The fact is, Señor Ríos, that you and I are true *exponents of energy.*"

"Indeed . . . ? Quite right. . . . Do you know, it had never occurred to me. However," continued Señor Ríos, raising his clenched fist to heaven, "I'd rather die of starvation than work for the Carranzistas!"

Don Rodolfo smiled indulgently.

"Those gentlemen have been a bit abrupt, for a fact, or, shall we say, unmannerly. Before we even had a chance to resign!"

"Precisely!" agreed Señor Ríos fiercely. "They threw us out just as you'd catch a cat by the tail and throw it into the creek!"

"They are more stupid than wicked. Even their chiefs are ignorant of the ABC's of political economy. Revolution is a certain means of making a fortune, just as government is the only means of preserving it and giving it a chance to grow as it deserves. Now, just as the rifle is indispensable in the first stage, so the office-holder is indispensable in the second. They think they can form a government by themselves, but they are only stones blown into the air which must inevitably come to earth again. But you and I represent an irresistible force, the force of inertia, and they must fall into our hands or destroy themselves in anarchy."

"Friend, you speak words of wisdom!"

The night, the silence, their excitement, drew them insensibly into the most daring confidences. They spoke in such low tones that one would say only their spirits were communing. Their words were finely shaded; their ideas hardly took form, but had a thousand nuances and imperceptible curves. They hesitated, backed, and side-stepped like blooded colts. What they finally gave each other to understand from all this tangle was something like the following.

"One of the rebel factions has already fallen into our hands. Villa and the bandits of his command are calling us back to our jobs. The bandits on the other side are doing the same."

"But," objected Señor Ríos, "Villa is a very dangerous man. They say his liver's as black as a jackal's."

"Just the same, the ex-federals will no longer be bothered with the services of the Gaucho Mojica. Villa took care of him. Do you understand me, Señor Ríos?"

"Aha! Is that what happened to him? Admirable! Sublime! You've made me very happy, Don Rodolfo!"

"It is painful that such energetic measures as those he practices have to be employed, but the rights of society are sacred. Bitter experience has taught us that it is only by such actions that our most illustrious statesmen have been able to purge our country of certain monsters."

"Public security is our first duty, Don Rodolfo. If you only knew! Why, I myself have signed the death warrants of innumerable criminals and, my friend, I swear to you that my pulse was quieter than it is at the present moment! I was only doing my duty like any honest public servant."

Perhaps because he had had nothing to eat, perhaps because of the frayed state of his nerves, Señor Ríos had an attack of the shakes that ended in a fit of blubbering.

"Why, oh my God," he thought, "why am I, Donaciano Ríos, an honest man to the marrow of my bones, why am I so tortured as a reward for my loyalty to my country, my home, and the faith of my fathers?"

Like a believer who has blasphemed, Señor Ríos began to tremble from head to foot. But this finished his strength and he fell exhausted into a heavy sleep that lasted till daybreak.

IV   REBIRTH

> *"The sun loosed his shafts of light over valley and mountain, bringing bird and beast and man to life."*—Garcilaso de la Vega

Dawn. A jeweled brush stroke flashed in the east. Gusts of cold air blew in through the open doors. A few sleepers stirred and grunted insults. Señor Ríos awoke puffing dryly like an asthmatic horse. Little by little the distant steel-colored hills began to take form. Masses of dark green and the bright houses of villages stood out. The cold grew more intense. More sleepers, their hair in disorder, their legs benumbed, sat up and rubbed their red eyes. They sighed dully.

The first rays of the sun flooded the valley with a

warm lake of gold. Scattered over the hills, the white and yellow houses looked like Christmas toys. The train slackened its speed on a grade. The village was plainly visible now and its people scurrying about. On a dunghill a cock with blood-red crest and flaming plumage lifted his head, beat his wings, and blew a crisp bugle call that shattered the air. Lowing cows with swollen udders put their muzzles over the fence of a corral.

The scene brightened faces and put a gleam of hope into tired eyes. No one asked questions; no one ventured a guess; no one commented. All were immersed in their own thoughts. Even Señor Ríos began to cherish the notion that his party might win out after all and that he might soon be home.

As the last shadows in the car were dissipated, new faces were recognized. Don Rodolfo pointed out several of his fellow townsmen to Señor Ríos. The fat gentleman who oozed grease from every pore and who snored even while standing, was Señor Rubalcaba, the principal of a state school and a wizard at reading old manuscripts and deciphering hieroglyphics. The gentleman with him was Don Sinforoso, mayor of Turicato. He also was rolling in fat, wore thick mustachios and had the face of a bulldog. A revolver and a knife stuck in his belt completed his get-up. Two jolly young women, heavily made up, served them as a kind of auxiliary force.

"And that young fellow over there, is he some ex-federal general?" asked Señor Ríos, impressed by the military bearing of a lad in highly polished leggings and a well fitting gray uniform, the whole set off by a fierce mustache and a rifle.

"I don't know him."

"He isn't a general," a stranger answered in a low voice. "He's only a tailor from my home town, Zamora."

"He looks it!" commented Señor Ríos, pleased.

"Have you noticed that pale young man who has just raised his head up there in front? The one with the big black eyes and chestnut curls? He's a lad with a great future—was a law student in the capital when the revolution struck. Neftalí! Neftalí! He can't hear me."

Don Rodolfo hopped over several sleepers.

"Neftalí, I want you to come back and meet a friend of mine, Señor Ríos."

"Does he draw any water?" asked the youth sadly.

"He's got lots of friends in the government."

"Well, in that case. . . ."

Neftalí half closed his girlish eyes and pursed his smooth lips. In three jumps they were back where Señor Ríos was absently observing the landscape.

"Señor Ríos, this is one of our most distinguished poets. Neftalí, Señor Ríos, state's attorney for Erongarícuaro, a rare soul and a particular friend of mine."

Neftalí bent his curly head and held out his manicured fingers.

"At the moment Neftalí is principal of the preparatory school of my state, a post which he occupies with great success and the satisfaction of his superiors. It is a pleasure to have two of my very best friends know each other."

Neither Señor Ríos nor Neftalí seemed particularly happy.

At the opposite end of the car, near the medicine closet, Marta, her children, and the doctor, were preparing to breakfast *en famille*. With the help of a bottle of mescal, Rubén, the major, and the doctor had managed to stay awake. They were still talking. The doctor opened a tin. Matilde broke an egg on the edge of the frying pan and complained of the nonsense she had had to listen to all night long. She turned the egg and looked at General Malacara, who was still lying flat on his back and snoring full blast. Matilde laughed and recited mockingly:

> *How nice, when you're sleepy, to sleep,*
> *And snore like a singing master!*
> *And eat and grow fat!*
> *And what a shame it is*
> *That that is not enough!*

"How well you read!"

"Do you act, Matilde?" asked the major. "What parts do you like best?"

"I cultivate art in all its branches. I play the violin, compose verses, write comedies, act in them, give readings. . . ."

"You haven't heard Matilde play the violin?" interrupted Marta excitedly. "She's divine! Why, we used to have regular recitals at our house and the governor himself honored us by attending!"

"Governor Izaguirre was so good to us!" sighed Matilde. "He almost lived at our house."

√ Rubén bit his lip. "You may not have noted," he was on the point of saying, "the remarkable resemblance of my sister Rosita to the governor. No wonder he was so good to us!" But a healthy respect for Matilde stopped his mouth.

Matilde, thrilling to her memories, turned the omelette nervously. She offered a slice of buttered toast and a cup of coffee to the doctor and went on with her story.

"That was the big day of my life! I wore a white tulle dress and satin slippers with silver heels. My hair was down over my breast and back and the Mexican flag was draped carelessly over one shoulder. Then the children from the state school marched in two by two and laid flowers at my feet, while the band played the national anthem. Oh, how everyone clapped!"

Matilde fell silent from sheer emotion. Rubén seized the opening.

"That was the day I got pinched and taken to the police station. One of the kids said: 'Look what a big nose she's got!' and I knocked him flat!"

The Reyes-Téllez annihilated Rubén with a glance.

"It was Matilde's greatest triumph," boasted Marta.

Whereupon, displaying a prodigious memory for her age, she gave a detailed description of that famous Sixteenth of September as it was written up in the local weekly.

"Señorita," said the doctor gravely, "please pardon my lack of modesty, but I'm going to ask the major there to fetch me some compositions of my own from the pine box yonder."

The major opened the pine box and returned laden with tins of sausages, ham, and the like, and was received with thunderous applause.

"The doctor's a wit!" exclaimed Rubén.

"What a doctor! And what a mistake we made judging you by our first impression!"

Everyone was enchanted.

Rosita had repaired the damage done to her face by the stormy night and was herself again. The doctor became very attentive. Matilde was trying to awaken the general with her chatter.

The noise made by the Reyes-Téllez and their friends stirred up less resentment in the car than the smell of their cooking. Don Sinforoso, who had already proclaimed three times that he was mayor of Turicato and a lieutenant colonel in the late federal army, could contain himself no longer.

"What a hell of a row!"

Señor Ríos begged him to lower his voice—the doctor and the major were officers in the sanitary corps.

"Well, what of it?"

"Nothing, except that we are traveling in their car. They haven't got very good manners, for a fact."

Don Sinforoso lighted a cigar and launched into a recital of the most stirring passages of his military career. The Zamora tailor and the other young dandies in uniform listened to him. Don Sinforoso was surrounded by ex-federals.

The doctor was very drunk. He overheard the word "federals" and jumped as if stung.

"The federals! That's what the fat herds of Porfirio Díaz, that fool De la Barra, and the bandit Huerta called themselves! The federals! Our purest national glory!"

Rubén was picking his teeth. He spat, looked timidly at Matilde, and ventured: "For our part we adored Señor Madero."

"Rosita," added Marta, "decorated a whole altar with flowers for poor little Señor Madero."

"Poor little Señor Madero? What imbecile said 'Poor little Señor Madero'? Poor little thing herself!"

So saying, the doctor collapsed on his bunk and fell sound asleep.

Don Sinforoso, who knew when to turn a deaf ear, took the floor again.

"After us federals," he said, "the Germans are the bravest soldiers on earth," and went on to sing their praises as reported in the latest bulletins from the western front.

While the Zamora tailor and the other military gentlemen were listening to the mayor of Turicato, Señor Ríos, who was at the end of his rope, begged his good friend Don Rodolfo not to introduce anyone else until they had had something to eat.

"But don't you want to hear Neftalí read his verses?"

Señor Ríos confessed honestly that at the moment he would prefer a dish of frijoles to all the literature in the world. But Don Rodolfo was merciless.

"Neftalí, read us 'A wild harmony swells my heart'. . . . What do you mean, you don't remember it? That lovely thing that begins: 'Lines written by Neftalí Sancho Peredo de la Garza to his beloved cousin Blanca.' "

"I can't recall a word of it, Don Rodolfo."

"Impossible! Why, it's one of your finest things!"

"Vain rhetoric, Señor Director. Platitudes."

"Allow me to differ with you. Those verses have life and truth."

"Life and truth have nothing to do with art," answered Neftalí, smiling.

"Your verses are full of harmony and sing the soul of things."

"The soul of things? Things haven't had a soul for some time past."

Don Rodolfo sought encouragement in the face of Señor Ríos, but encountered only a black scowl. Señor Ríos was looking at the young poet as he might have contemplated the Sphinx.

"Did you two eat last night?" he demanded.

"At ten thirty," answered Don Rodolfo in alarm.

As he spoke, a voice from the other end of the car said: "Señor Ríos, won't you have a bite with us?"

And Señor Ríos was off like a shot.

V VICTIM OF THE REVOLUTION

One of General Malacara's girls was speaking.

"Manuela, sit up! You can see Irapuato from here!"

Manuela stirred heavily, mumbled something un-intelligible, and sat up. Still befuddled, she pulled away the hair that was sticking to her damaged make-up, looked around, got to her feet and went to the door to take her bearings. Shielding her swollen eyes from the glare, little by little she made out the lead-colored roofs of the distant station.

"Tell me, Cachucha, is that smoke, or am I still asleep?"

The two girls looked with interest toward the south where, beyond the dense, dun-colored mesquite slashed by the dazzling white ballast of the roadbed, a leaden cloud was rising above the green groves of Irapuato. The train rounded a sharp curve and the cloud unexpectedly became a multitude of twisting columns of black smoke which melted together in a sooty canopy.

"It's Villa's trains, Cachucha!"

"It's Villa's trains, Manuela!"

Señor Ríos heard their cries and felt his heart turn over and squeeze itself dry. His teeth chattered. Villa's trains! He saw it all now, but how could he break the news to Don Rodolfo? Were they not, indeed, exponents of energy, as Don Rodolfo had sworn? This must be the appointed hour in which to put their high qualities to the test. Señor Ríos told him what he had heard, betraying his intense emotion only by his heavy breathing and by hitching his trousers up higher than usual.

"My canary! Where's my canary? Merciful heaven! Has anyone seen my canary? This is God's punishment on me for neglecting my darling! Please, gentlemen, haven't you seen my canary?"

Matilde's distress went unnoticed. As they approached Irapuato all busied themselves collecting their bags and valises. Rosita did her hair and those who had nothing to carry dusted themselves off and did the same. Irapuato! The end of the run! Irapuato! Breakfast! Lodging! A bed! Sheets! Happiness!

The train stopped in the open country and bunches of benumbed humanity clinging to the roof of the cars began to drop off. They got to the ground, stretched their arms and legs, and scattered, some toward the yellow battlements of a hacienda that could be seen above the mesquite; others set off in single file down the dusty paths of the track toward the station.

"You, boy! What's the train stopping here for?"

A soldier in white pants and muddy boots, rifle on shoulder, looked foolishly up at the mayor of Turicato and walked on without answering.

"I asked you, idiot, why is the train stopping here?" repeated Don Sinforoso arrogantly.

The soldier stopped. His face like an Aztec mask stared stupidly up at the ex-federal.

"You'd like to know, would you? Me too."

"Do you know who you're talking to, blockhead?"

"Well, I don't think I'm talking to my father, because my father wasn't a ——!"

At the soldier's epithet the mayor's auxiliaries covered their ears, while Don Sinforoso proved to everyone's satisfaction that his vocabulary was richer than the soldier's. He put his hand furiously to his pistol. Moralitos, Señor Ríos, Don Rodolfo, and Neftalí prudently left the line of fire, trampling the passengers, and took refuge in the corner where Moralitos' grandmother was installed.

"Take it easy!" said Señor Ríos nervously. "It isn't funny to play with firearms!"

"Something could easily go wrong," the old woman agreed.

"My mother-in-law got killed with a pistol holster," observed a joker.

"We'll see, dolt, whether you can be taught how to address an officer!" said Don Sinforoso, drawing his pistol.

Without changing his expression, the soldier shifted the butt of his rifle to his shoulder. The auxiliaries screamed and threw themselves upon the colonel. The schoolmaster, whose corpulence prevented his making a heroic gesture, contented himself with taking Don Sinforoso's hand, ever so gently.

"You are asking for trouble, colonel."

Señor Rubalcaba felt such slight resistance in the colonel's fingers that he took it as an invitation and disarmed him with all due courtesy and respect. Thereupon Don Sinforoso frothed with rage and aired his feelings with a wealth of invective, while the tailor and the schoolmaster bore him out of range. Wild with fury and chewing his words, Don Sinforoso said that only his regard for the fair sex had prevented his making a horrible example of the soldier.

The soldier, still wearing his idiotic look, walked slowly away, after paying his respects to the colonel and all his family. When he was out of sight Moralitos sprang from his hiding place into the middle of the car.

"Unbelievable! What discipline!" And then, in Don Sinforoso's ear: "Is it possible, colonel, that this rabble defeated our glorious federal army?"

"The federal army, my friend, was never defeated! We were betrayed! With a handful of men I put hundreds of these ragamuffins to flight!"

"Yes, colonel, but this time you would have got the worst of it."

They were interrupted by a piercing shriek. Matilde had just discovered her cage and the canary smashed flat under a pile of saddles. Subconsciously Matilde sensed that her scream had transcended the merely beautiful and attained the sublime. Her grief revealed depths of feeling hitherto unsuspected even by herself, and she let herself go and did the whole chromatic scale of pain, while Moralitos caught her as she fainted in his arms.

VI THE GENERAL

General Malacara was the last one to come to. He sat up, unglued his heavy eyelids, and flashed his teeth. He stretched his arms and legs, yawned, and explored the car, now half empty, for hunger had forced many to get off and forage. He noticed Marta and her daughters, and, as if just recollecting something very important, rose and greeted them.

"Ah, general," said Marta, "were you in this car too?"

Rosita, absently gazing at the landscape, offered him a limp hand.

"And Matilde?"

Rubén told him of the disaster to the canary. Poor little Matilde was in a corner, her head wrapped in a black shawl, sobbing unconsolably.

"Child, there's no use in that. Better thank God. Less trouble for the journey."

"Will you have a cup of coffee, general?"

The doctor, still half asleep, made shift to light the alcohol lamp, but Matilde jumped to her feet.

"No, doctor, no! The very idea! Not while there are women about. After all the favors and attentions we owe you? *We* have some manners and know how to treat decent people!"

Matilde's glance was acid and her words were bitter, but she heated the general's coffee and fried his eggs with her own hands.

"Bermúdez! Bermúdez! Bring some beer."

A bumpkin in an enormous sombrero, sleeping on a pile of luggage, bestirred himself, poked about, and came up with several bottles of beer. But the general was thoroughly snubbed, except for Rubén, who was always agreeable, and Bermúdez, who never refused a drink. His defeat, however, did not stand in the way of his devouring his breakfast, while Rosita, at a safe distance from him, struck up a conversation with the doctor. Still foggy with sleep, the doctor asked her if the general was a relative.

"He's only a friend, a friend of the family . . . and, you know, there are friends and friends. You, for example, we met only yesterday, but you won us immediately with your gentlemanly manners, with your air of distinction. Everything about you showed that you are a respectable person. So we have been true friends since yesterday, because our friendship is unselfish and noble and not just on the surface. We liked each other and that was that. But take a look at the other side of the picture. Take my case. A decent person of good family, with aristocratic connections, is poor and has to work for a living. So she has to make friends in the official world, and the first thing she knows she has picked up acquaintances . . . well, you can imagine the kind of scum! People beneath her, no manners or anything. You understand, don't you?"

The doctor understood pretty well. Rosita was laughing loudly, shrugging her shoulders, tossing her neat little head, swaying her hips, and putting out one small foot to display the beginning of a firm round leg.

"So the general is one of your suitors, is he?" the doctor asked abruptly.

"Lord! What an idea! Isn't that just like a man? General Malacara a suitor of mine!"

Rosita's high laughter did the scales.

"What nonsense! I must look like a scarecrow if that's what you think of me! Why, doctor, he's old enough to be my grandfather!"

Rosita glanced down at herself, twisted about coquettishly, and trilled like a wild bird. The general finally got the point and went to speak to Matilde.

"Do you know those girls who are with me?"

"We're not greatly interested in knowing them, general."

"Tut, tut, child! They are only two poor youngsters from my part of the country, friends of mine, practically relatives. They weren't able to get back to Durango, eh? Naturally, I offered to get them home. You know how it is. Very nice girls. I've known 'em ever since they were so high. They like a nip now and then," added the general confidentially, "just like you, just like me, just like everybody, eh? Outside of that they're very nice girls."

The general was warming up to his subject. He suggested that he would like to bring them over and introduce them.

"Let me bring 'em over. You'll like 'em. I want you to be friends . . . close friends. We'll all be like one family. . . . As I told you, they're practically relatives . . . distant."

Rubén was about to chime in with his ritualistic "It will be a pleasure, general," when Matilde, red as a cock's comb, gave the general to understand it wouldn't do at all.

A gang of track hands, white with dust, approached the hospital car. Moralitos, his handkerchief knotted about his neck, his face flushed and contorted, his eyes like hard-boiled eggs, spread the alarm. The train had stopped because the track was cut! A disaster! The trains of the Northern Division had steam up, all ready for the retreat! A disaster!

"What's that busybody yelling about?" said the general, going to the door. "Will you shut up, fool, or shall I have you shot? Too many chickens around here!"

A pale hush spread through the car. In the midst of it came a solemn croaking.

"Friends, Francisco Villa has not been defeated, nor can he be defeated. His fate is not in human hands. It is written: Mexico will burn in horrible revolutions, and hunger will come, and plagues, and war. . . . Four Franciscos will rule over us. The prophecy must be fulfilled: Francisco León de la Barra, Francisco Madero, Francisco Carbajal. . . . Only one is left, Francisco Villa. It is written!"

The pythoness turned out to be Moralitos' grandmother. Everyone waited.

"And then?" asked Marta, shivering.

"Ah, and then! Three messengers will come, and the first will say: 'All is lost!' And the second will go his way without a word. And the third will be of fire and water, and he will say: 'All is saved!' And the victory of the Church will be such as has never been seen! And the Americans will bring over the King of Spain, and he will reign over us, and all will obey the will of God!"

The old woman fell silent. Her voice was solemn, her expression sacerdotal. The doctor burst into an impious laugh. Marta and her children were thoughtful. Señor Ríos and his friends turned away without comment and set off for Irapuato. Neftalí rolled up his trousers, pulled down the brim of his hat, grasped his cane, and, gravely and ceremoniously, brought up the rear of the procession.

"Children," said the general, "I propose that we go and see Irapuato. We'll die of boredom here. This is going to last a long time. Bermúdez, have my car unloaded."

Marta's and Matilde's integrity suffered a heavy strain. Only to think of seeing Irapuato in the general's car! But Rosita saved them.

"We're sorry, general, but the doctor has already done us the honor of inviting us. We can't be rude to him."

The doctor did not try to hide his astonishment, at which the major and the general laughed heartily.

"Well, then, Manuela and Cachucha, get yourselves ready. We're going for a ride to Irapuato."

The general's porcelain teeth glistened in the half light of the car.

VII   VADE RETRO

*"Plumes there are that can cross a morass
and never show a spot. . . ."*
—Díaz Mirón

"Good Lord! Are we going in *that?*"

Matilde's face hardened when the doctor indicated the dray he had hired to take them to the city. Even Rosita felt her face burning when she saw Bermúdez and several soldiers easing the general's big gray car down an inclined plane to the ground. The general and his girls waited calmly in the shade of a tree.

"You damned old women!" raged Rubén.

"Of course!" answered Matilde bravely. "But our dignity comes first."

"We must preserve our dignity," chorused the rest of the family solemnly.

"Run now! No one's looking!" cried Marta, making a dash for the dray.

Rosita waited until the general and his girls had their backs turned, and ran and took her place.

"Nicomedes, bring the shopping bags," ordered the doctor. "Things look bad, young ladies, and we don't know how long we may be stuck in the desert. We've got to stock up with provisions."

Faces softened at the doctor's thoughtfulness.

"But," said Marta, "I still don't believe in Villa's defeat."

"You doubt it?"

Rubén and Matilde exchanged uneasy glances. Marta began to tremble.

"You'll have to look up your friend Quiñones, Rubén, as we planned."

"Where do you think I could find him now, sister?"

"You don't have to be very smart to find a schoolmaster!"

In the long silence their faces reflected their anxiety. The doctor was the first to recover.

"Well, we're going to have a pleasant ride. The trees are beautiful and it's cool."

The only response he got was a grunt from Rubén. Even Rosita, as she was bumped along the road, seemed to share the stunned silence of the birds in the branches oppressed by the heat.

As they neared Irapuato they overtook the soldiers' women, the *soldaderas*, ragged and exhausted. Black and smoky huts lined the road. Sooty faces peered from doorways with sad, frightened eyes. Everywhere, uneasiness and anxiety.

They entered the town by a white, powdery lane between thatched huts with roofs rotted by the rain and scorched by the sun. At a cross street near the market they came upon a group of grimy women talking and gesticulating who fell silent as statues when the dray passed. Only their staring eyes and long necks followed the group until it was out of sight.

Rubén questioned the passers-by at random. Villa's defeat was the only thing they could talk about. Irapuato was being evacuated. The troops at the station were waiting to be entrained. The enemy were so close that at any moment now one would be able to hear the firing between Villa's rear guard and Obregón's van.

"Old wives' tales!" said Rubén valiantly, but his heart was in his throat.

And it was said that the enemy were committing every kind of atrocity, with no respect for women, children, or old people! They carried a flag with the skull and crossbones on it! They were killing people as one would step on ants!

"Exaggerations! Ridiculous!" protested Marta.

The dray moved on. Its riders were indignant at the gullibility of the people, but they were silent and worried.

Ahead it was worse. Carts and carriages piled high with trunks, mattresses, furniture, and humanity were moving in all directions. Public buildings were being emptied. Government clerks were coming and going, meeting and mingling, dazed, unable to sense the magnitude of the catastrophe.

In the main street Matilde noticed the bony flanks and the legs, bent like springs, of their sweating, mangy nag. Very red in the face, not so much from the heat as from the embarrassment she suddenly felt, she cried: "Well, what are we staying up here for?"

They all got down.

"While we do some shopping, Ruben, you go and find your friend Quiñones. We'll meet in the square later."

Rubén glanced about and marched off without a word. Rosita walked ahead of the doctor. Matilde comforted Marta, who was so overcome she couldn't swallow.

"Come, Mama! Now you're being really silly! We've got plenty of friends among the Carranzistas. If the Villistas fall, we'll fall too, but we'll fall on our feet! Cheer up! Quiñones will save us."

The marketplace was bursting with people. Soldiers and peasants milled about the doors, some struggling to get in, others, their baskets full, fighting to get out. Shouts, insults, an occasional slap.

One skinny and sickly looking soldier, convinced of the hopelessness of trying to get through, leaned against a wall, and gnawed a withered carrot with doggish single-mindedness.

Rosita gave up the struggle too and amused herself by looking over the dusty stands of rotted cloth and the tables loaded with useless gimcracks.

They finally escaped from the market, Nicomedes with his baskets filled with spongy cabbages, wilted lettuce, huge chunks of beef, cheeses and pieces of butter wrapped in corn husks. In one hand Marta carried a shopping bag bursting with greens and eggs, and in the other a bunch of chickens, head downward, clucking, half suffocated.

"Doctor, you must tell us what our share is. . . . Of course you will! It's only right. As soon as Rubén returns we'll pay you. But where is Rosita? Confound the girl! As usual we've got to look for her everywhere."

"There she is!"

The doctor indicated the show windows of a shoe shop called The Jockey Club.

"Oh Mama! See what nice boots for the trip! I

could save my patent leather slippers for the street. If we could only draw a two weeks' advance I'd buy them right now."

"It isn't necessary, Rosita. Rubén has enough money. Only by the time he gets here the boots will be gone. Just look at the crowd in there!"

The doctor gallantly offered his services. The trouble was that Matilde had found another pair that couldn't fit her better if they had been made to order. What a pity that Rubén was so long in returning!

But the doctor, who had already spent 250 pesos, Villa paper, turned his wallet inside out.

"But, doctor, as soon as Rubén gets here we'll pay you back to the last cent!"

The doctor bit his lip with annoyance and made no reply.

It happened that as they were leaving the shoe shop the gray car was passing. They caught a glimpse of gaudy clothes and the white teeth and waving hand of General Malacara. Matilde's face turned leaden. Rosita's make-up had dissolved in the sun, dust, and wind. This, rather than any emotion, gave her a look of ill temper. Marta scowled and thrust out her lips like the spout of a vinegar cruet.

"A pretty friend we picked up! You can't imagine, Rosita, how hard it is for me to keep my mouth shut!"

"But only think! If those . . . uh . . . females saw us riding in that cart! What could we have been thinking of, Matilde?"

"Don't talk to me! I feel the blood of the Reyes-Téllez rushing to my head and I won't answer for myself!"

Matilde turned abruptly to the doctor and offered her hand.

"Doctor, we're sorry we can't go any farther with you, but we'd forgotten we had a call to make."

"I understand," answered the doctor coolly, taking her hand.

Nicomedes went to pick up the bag of provisions and the bunch of chickens, but Marta protested.

"What are you doing? The doctor will be paid for everything. But this is ours. We bought it ourselves."

"The very idea!" she went on, when the doctor and Nicomedes were out of range. "Who would have paid me for getting my corns stepped on and all the work of picking those things out?"

"Bah! A little pill-roller who does his own shopping!"

"And who can't afford an automobile!"

"And who hasn't even got 200 Villa pesos in his pocket!"

"This has been perfectly ridiculous! I do hope that nobody we know saw us!"

"He's just the type I can't abide!"

The three women had lost their way when the general's car reappeared in the distance.

"He's alone!" cried Rosita excitedly.

"*They* aren't with him!" echoed Matilde with her heart in her mouth.

"Come, Rosita, Mama! Don't turn around. Act as though nothing has happened."

The three continued on their way calmly.

"And Rubén, Mama?"

"He has probably got things all fixed up. They are

old school friends and very fond of each other. Quiñones wrote him that one of our professors is now a Carranzista general and he has great hopes of finding a good job if they win."

"Matilde, don't you think in that case it would be better to break with General Malacara and get it over with?"

"What's the hurry? Quite the contrary. We've got to get him to introduce us to General Villa, as he promised."

"Well, they do say that General Villa is very kind and that all you've got to do with him is to cry and he'll give you anything."

"Moralitos told me," Marta was talking with great animation now, "Moralitos told me that he spoke to General Villa at the time of the Aguascalientes Convention and got 500 pesos out of him, and they were worth the same as silver in those days. And he got a pass to Ciudad Juárez for twelve people that he sold for 200, and a complete uniform, with hat and coat, and a pair of genuine American shoes! We'll leave the passes for the last. That's the easiest part. First we'll ask him for corn, sugar, rice, flour, blankets, and a hat and several pairs of shoes for Rubén. After that the money and the passes. Don't you think so, Matilde?"

"And what good do you think his money will do us if nobody will take it?" demanded Rosita.

"Don't be silly! We can throw it away when it gets us as far as León or Aguascalientes. Rubén will stay behind with Quiñones and by the time we get back there'll be jobs for all of us and we'll have nothing to do but move in."

"Oh, how do you do, general?"

"I was looking for you, children."

"To be sure, general. Whenever you like . . . alone. We're your friends, your very dear friends, but don't ask impossibilities."

"We just couldn't! You know us. We Reyes-Téllez have always been a bit choosy."

"All right, all right," smiled the general. "But what happened to our doctor?"

"Oh, he's a good enough sort, but Lord, what a bore! Simply unbearable. Of course, he was so nice to us that it would have been bad manners not to accept his invitation, but we got rid of him as soon as we could."

"We gave him the air."

"So coarse!"

"So pig-headed!"

"So stingy!"

"Why, just imagine, general! He couldn't even lend us the 200 pesos we needed for a pair of boots at The Jockey Club. They'd have been so useful for me on the trip."

"Just like these I bought," put in Matilde. "Only Rubén has got our money and we had only enough for one pair."

"They're pretty clumsy," observed the general, comparing them with Rosita's patent leather slippers, "but if they're good enough for Matilde let's go buy 'em."

They were just entering The Jockey Club when Rubén appeared, beaming.

"I saw Quiñones! He sent you his best and will be

waiting for us at his house at three. Everything's fixed!"

"General," said Marta, "we'd like to remind you of your promise to introduce us to General Villa."

"Anything you like," answered General Malacara, with his unfailing good fellow's smile.

Rosita tried on her boots. Rubén asked to be shown a pair of yellow leather leggings, stiff and bright as sheet copper.

"They're magnificent!"

"Try them on, Rubén," urged Rosita. "Go on! You'll look very handsome in them. They fit you perfectly! You look just like a federal officer! For goodness' sake buy them, Rubén!"

"I left the house in such a hurry that I forgot my money in the pocket of my other coat, as you know perfectly well."

"What are the leggings worth?" asked the general, with unflagging good humor.

The leggings were not dear, for a fact, only 350 pesos, but there was always the danger that within five minutes they might be worth 500 or 1000, depending upon the speed at which Villa paper depreciated. Rubén could repay all that and more with a few advances on his salary. Besides, Marta, Matilde, and Rosita, particularly Rosita, all offered to guarantee the debt. The general made the clerk repeat the price, called him a thief, and tossed him a roll of bills without taking the trouble to count them— which had the effect of kicking the poor fellow in the belly.

"What a difference!" whispered the Reyes-Téllez. "This is a real friend!"

Their eyes spoke volumes as they climbed into the automobile. The general took the wheel and put Rosita on his right. Matilde sank into the leather cushions of the tonneau with all the indolence of a duchess.

"General, we wish you could get us into another car, the governor's, for instance. Our little doctor has joggled us into a poultice with his dray. . . . Imagine! He had the nerve to make a play for Rosita! Ha, ha, ha!"

"Especially, general . . . you know us . . . he hardly belongs. You will take us to the governor's car, won't you, general?"

The general nodded, but at the moment he was giving more attention to steering the automobile and to the little game he was playing with Rosita's feet.

Rubén, with the arrogance of a minister of state, ignored the friends they passed on the street.

Heavy trucks, crowded with women and soldiers, roared by. Sunburned, bewhiskered, and beslobbered faces, mingled with painted ones, showed above the sides. Below, heavy, mud-covered boots flirted with high-heeled shoes.

All this gave Matilde the opportunity to make comparisons. Her thought slipped neatly into a verse which she recited in her rich voice.

"Plumes there are that can cross a morass
And never show a spot. . . ."

Our plumage is like that, General Malacara."

VIII MR. SECRETARY!

General Malacara was a good sort, but fickle. They had hardly reached the station when he began to cast about for some way to get rid of his charges, and all because he had glimpsed, in the half open window of a house on the Avenida Juárez, a pair of very black eyes, a copper skin, a noble bust, and a wink.

"Children, while you are waiting to meet General Villa you might take the opportunity to talk with the Secretary of Public Instruction who has just come in from the north. He could be of some help to you."

"Of course!" exclaimed Matilde, delighted. "Rubén can get some advances on his salary as an employee of the department. Yes, yes, of course! Let's go see the secretary at once."

"Here's a card for him and one for General Villa. In case I'm not back at the station when the general arrives, my card will get you in immediately."

"And where shall we see you afterward?"

"Right here, at five."

"Don't forget your promise. We'll all travel in the governor's car, won't we?" said Matilde, already on her way to the secretary's car.

They mounted a platform and were received by a foolish-looking ox-like youth who exuded alcohol from his very eyes. Rosita presented the general's card, which he took drunkenly, along with Rosita's hand. His eyes devoured her.

"This way."

They took seats in the tiny compartment that did duty for a reception room. The youth disappeared into the adjoining one. Rosita hastily powdered her nose, arranged the curls on her forehead, poked up those on her neck, and opened carelessly, ever so little, the lace of her blouse, barely enough to give a hint of the whiteness and softness there concealed, just as a bit of heaven might be seen through a chink in a window.

A typewriter clacked monotonously.

More civilians entered. Rubén recognized a friend and got up to greet him. Rubén asked him what he knew about the secretary.

"The only thing I know about him is that he handled the propaganda for the Madero-Pino Suárez crowd in Guadalajara."

Rubén thanked him and reported to Matilde.

"He was a journalist, speaker, or something or other, in Guadalajara, during the time of the idiot Madero."

"I get it."

A small green curtain opened and a yellow wrinkled face behind glasses peered at them obliquely and disappeared.

"What was that ugly thing, Rosita?"

"An angora cat."

"A gorilla with goggles."

When the drunken youth opened the door and beckoned them in, it turned out that the cat, or gorilla, was none other than the secretary himself. He was lying stretched out on a couch, his socks down about his ankles, vest unbuttoned, glasses on nose.

Without bothering to raise his eyes from his book, he asked:

"Well, what do you want?"

Matilde flushed to the roots of her hair. The phlegmatic Rubén measured his words.

"Mr. Secretary, we only wished to have the honor of presenting our most profound respects to you as employees of the Department of Public Instruction."

"And at the same time," added Matilde, with emphasis, "to express our utmost admiration for your revolutionary effort and your noble political career."

"Especially, Mr. Secretary, for your brilliant speeches."

"Me? Speeches?" interrupted the secretary, lowering his book at last. "You're raving, my young friend. I never made a speech in my life."

"Please excuse him, Mr. Secretary. My brother is very shy and gets things mixed. What he had in mind was the brilliant editorials you wrote in Guadalajara during the administration of our glorious martyr, Señor Madero."

"To be sure, to be sure. I did condescend to write for the newspapers."

"But what particularly pleased us was that your articles didn't seem to have been written by a newspaperman at all! They were something different!"

"Do you really think so, my young friends? Well, well, that's just what I've always said. Certainly."

Monkey-like, the secretary's scowl disappeared in a smile of infantile delight.

"So you're from Guadalajara?"

"We lived in Guadalajara at the time. We were always mad about Señor Madero. . . ."

"As we are now about General Villa."

"And his distinguished colleagues."

Matilde and Rubén were racing to cap each other's thoughts.

"That is why, Mr. Secretary, we joined the party that represents the honorable, the healthy, the noble side of the revolution."

"And that is why, Mr. Secretary, we chose to suffer the loss of our home, the bitterness of exile, the hardships of a wandering life, rather than serve thieves."

"Because, Mr. Secretary, that's precisely what those accursed Carranzistas are!"

"Certainly, certainly," answered the secretary, wiping his glasses and staring idiotically at Rosita. "Jalisco is pretty, certainly! Don't worry, my young friends. I know what you came for. Timoteo! Timoteo-o-o! Don't worry, my young friends. Schoolteachers are not in demand at the moment, but we do need help in the hospitals. Timoteo, take these young people to my old friend General Tlacuache and tell him I'm sending them to him. Don't worry, my young friends. At least you won't die of hunger."

"But, Mr. Secretary. . . ."

"Congratulations, my young friends, congratulations!"

The secretary stood up, shook hands with them effusively and with his free hand pushed them out the door.

"Stupid old fool!" whispered Rubén, as soon as they were outside.

"Old gorilla!" fumed Matilde.

"Never mind, officer. You needn't bother with

escorting us. General Villa will take care of us. We really don't need anybody's recommendations."

They rejoined Marta, who was guarding the bags, the provisions, and the chickens.

IX UNWELCOME ENCOUNTER

"Poor Señor Rubalcaba! He's so fat and it's so hot!" exclaimed Raquel, the fifth-grade teacher. She was small, had a turned-up nose, prominent chin, and voluptuous eyes.

Raquel was on Don Sinforoso's arm.

"For goodness' sake, Aurora," she called to her companion, "lend poor Señor Rubalcaba your arm. You've left him all alone."

Aurora, the fourth-grade teacher, was walking between the Zamora tailor and the other young officer. She made a face, but came forward and offered her arm to Señor Rubalcaba. The schoolmaster was jealous and scolded her, but she soon brought him round.

"No, Señor Rubalcaba, you're quite wrong. They're both ex-federals and very nice."

The schoolmaster wiped his face with a huge checked handkerchief and drew a deep breath. His eyes were almost popping out of their sockets.

"I'm dying, I don't know whether from hunger or fatigue."

He had been walking for an interminable hour through the dust in the broiling sun and still could not even see the roof of the Irapuato station. There

was no break in the string of trains. The steel boilers
and red cars reflected the heat. Underneath, lying
on their bellies between the wheels, engineers, con-
ductors, and brakemen, black with soot, slept.

"God, how my feet hurt! Friend, give me a drink,
will you?"

The tailor dropped his heavy rifle, took a bottle of
tequila out of his hip pocket, and passed it to his
companion.

"After you."

"Your health."

"And yours."

"If it's true that Villa is licked, then I'm cooked."

"Well, how about me?"

"They got a diamond ring out of me. Imagine
that!"

"They got my gold watch and a three piece chamois
skin hunting outfit with silver buttons and gold
braid."

"I can't see that you lost anything to fall dead
over. If I had your tailor shop in Zamora I wouldn't
have a care in the world."

"At this moment my shop in Zamora is probably a
Carranzista pigsty and my goods are horse blankets.
The only things you need, on the other hand, are
your desk and what you've got in your head."

"My desk hasn't brought me in a cursed cent in six
months. Since that riffraff came to Zamora there
hasn't been a crust of bread in the house. Give me
that bottle!"

"Here's to you."

"Here's hoping we get out of this."

"Still," said the notary, after a moment's reflection, "the fact is I didn't give General Marañón that diamond ring just to get something out of him. I liked him, that's all. That's the way I am with my friends."

"Of course," replied the tailor. "It's the same with me. May I drop dead this minute if I didn't give him my gold watch and my chamois skin hunting outfit with the silver buttons and gold braid just because I loved him so!"

The tailor heaved a sigh from his very boots.

"Let's have another."

"Let's."

"Here's to friendship!"

They fell silent. They could hear nothing but the vague noises of the town and, now and then, distant shots. Even the sparrows were quiet in the brush. From along the track, where the hundred trains were strung out, a thick dirty smudge rose into the turquoise sky.

"Time to be getting along," said the notary.

They shouldered their rifles and trudged on in silence. The alcohol was beginning to take effect.

"It will be a joke on us if we've been backing the wrong horse."

They sighed. At intervals one of them uttered a monosyllable, which the other matched. They understood each other.

"What wouldn't I give for a little government job for a couple of months!"

"My uncle Dionisio was custodian of rural property for a mere thirty days and came out of it with a house and a farm."

"A friend of mine named Serapio Lechuga walked off with some jewels worth a hundred thousand, gold!"

"He was smart. Went with the Carranza crowd."

"That's the real racket, my friend."

"This star I've got on my hat has brought me nothing but bad luck."

"Well," said the notary, now very drunk, "the truth is I didn't get this commission out of the general just so I could go out on the road and hold up defenseless people."

"That would have been dumb—for a notary."

"Or a tailor!"

"Do you mean to call me a thief?"

"Well, what are you calling me?"

Both grasped their rifles, but happened to raise their heads at the same moment. They stared at each other for a space, grinned, and put out their hands.

"It was just a drunken notion."

"Don't mind me, friend."

Señor Ríos and his companions were fainting with hunger. In vain they stopped at every hut they came to; all had been stripped clean. They left the road hopelessly and walked over to a shack that looked like a haystack from a distance. A tattered old woman came to the door. She turned them away. Discouraged, they were walking back when they met Don Sinforoso, Señor Rubalcaba, and the auxiliaries.

"Find anything to eat?"

"Not even a drop of water," answered Moralitos, on the verge of tears.

The old woman's cruelty infuriated Don Sinforoso. "We'll teach the old bitch to trifle with an ex-federal!"

In a voice of thunder he ordered her to bring out instantly all the provisions in the house and, without waiting for her excuses, he drew his pistol. Bang, bang, bang! The bullets crashed against the hard mud walls until the pistol was empty. The old woman threw up her hands and displayed her toothless gums. Her eyes bugged out with terror. While Señor Rubalcaba and the auxiliaries dashed gourdfuls of water on the fire that had started in the thatch, the old woman opened a cupboard and brought out a large pot of atole and a sack of limp and leathery tortillas.

The bitter atole and the tortillas made a delicious repast. Strength returned. Smiles appeared. Life wasn't so bad after all. Señor Rubalcaba caught Aurora of the fourth grade off her guard and kissed her on the neck. The firm cheeks of Raquel of the fifth grade received the impact of Don Sinforoso's bristly lips. Nor did it stop there. . . .

They set out again for the station, with Señor Ríos well to the rear. At every fresh outrage to his morals he raised his eyes to heaven and noted the direction of the columns of smoke in the cloudless sky.

At the station, which they neared at long last, the tide of humanity washed up to their feet. On every hand they saw ragged and sick-looking soldiers, women all skin and bones, angry and despairing faces. Soon they could push their way through the boiling mass of people only with difficulty. The station was bursting with officialdom. A constant stream of generals, colonels, and other field officers flowed in and out of the telegraph office, which was clicking incessantly.

Outside, in the square, the stands were folding their white awnings. Only a little while before, the market place had been the center of a merry riot of soldiers and peasants, and the plebeian strains of "Adelita" executed by the noisy brass of the town band had mingled with the muffled notes of a street orchestra, the scraping of fiddles, the monotonous grinding of hand organs, and the tuneless songs of drunks and prostitutes. It was now rapidly becoming the picture of desolation.

The Carranzistas! Panic blanched the faces of civilians. The pink cheeks of the ex-federal officers registered annoyance. Those of the pure Indians of the Northern Division showed nothing whatever.

The heavy smoke of the hundred trains blackened the sky. Safety valves hissed and sputtered stridently. Noses, mouths, and ears were filled with smoke. Smoke penetrated pores and reddened eyes. Everything reeked of sulphur.

Don Sinforoso felt a sudden and imperious urge and begged to be excused. He crawled under the couplings between two cars and was lost to view. He had hardly pitched camp when he sensed the presence, at no great distance, of a soldier similarly engaged. In the middle of the operation the soldier had the unhappy notion to look up and found himself face to face with his neighbor. Don Sinforoso had a sudden cramp. Christ! It was the same soldier he had rowed with that morning! Still squatting, Don Sinforoso bowed and gave the soldier a most polite and amiable salute. The soldier was overjoyed.

"Good work, my lad!" said Don Sinforoso, not too heartily. "I recognized you. You're the one who wouldn't take a calling down this morning. That's the kind of man I want! With a hundred like you I wouldn't leave a Carranzista alive!"

Don Sinforoso felt he had achieved a diplomatic triumph. He called a short truce, lost his cramp, and arose, very red in the face.

"I was a bit rough on you this morning," he added, buttoning his trousers, "but I was just trying you out and learned that you're a real man. I'll tell General Villa about you. Come, give me your hand."

He seized the calloused paw of the soldier and shook it vigorously. The soldier made no resistance.

But another surprise was in store for Don Sinforoso, a very painful one. Grouped closely together at a safe distance, Señor Ríos and his party, the schoolmaster and the auxiliaries, were watching the scene in alarm.

"Are you all right?" called Moralitos.

"We saw that man's face between the cars," said Raquel, "and we ran to protect you."

"We were going to scream if he made a move," added Aurora.

"But you're so pale!" said Señor Ríos, genuinely concerned. "Did anything serious happen?"

The auxiliaries embraced Don Sinforoso effusively and shed real tears.

"Bah!" exploded the colonel. "Will you let me get in a word? What the devil! The poor wretch hardly recognized me when he began to shake like a poisoned cur. Yes, sir! I could have had him shot if I had felt like it, but these poor ignorant fools. . . .

I'm sorry for them. It's no fault of theirs. Anyway, I'm too soft-hearted to do my duty very often. 'It's all right, friend,' I said. 'I'm not going to hurt you.' He was too scared to understand me. He couldn't stand up and, just to reassure him, I shook hands with him. And that was all there was to it!"

X RESPECTABLE PEOPLE

"Let's go in here," said Don Sinforoso, pushing open the door of the station restaurant. "I see a good many ex-federals. They're all decent people. We might get something to eat and find out what it's all about."

The tables were filled with men in correct gray uniforms, new hats, polished boots and leggings.

Raquel and Aurora entered, somewhat timidly. A young, pink-cheeked officer jumped up and offered them his place. His neighbor, a major with yellow mustaches, bloodshot eyes, and a red handkerchief about his neck, did the same. The rest pushed back their chairs and welcomed the newcomers cordially. The young officer excused himself and went to serve them.

Don Sinforoso launched into a long account of his exploits which was so interesting that the nearest officers crowded round him to hear better and, incidentally, to be leg to leg with the auxiliaries. These sighed with satisfaction, almost with delight. The officers were *so* hospitable and polite.

Don Sinforoso led the conversation.

"It was like a panic in a hen coop when a coyote breaks in," remarked an old major, who was something of a wit.

"They can't fight," asserted another gravely. "This famous Northern Division and its mighty deeds are all bluff. The proof of it is that when our federals attacked them we lost only our ammunition train. And our men were nothing but rabbits! Conscripts! The only thing they thought of was running or deserting to the enemy. Villa bagged them just as if he were out hunting!"

"Well, what I say," put in another, "is that if they hadn't faked our countersign they'd never have broken our line."

"What line are you talking about?" interrupted the major with the red handkerchief and the yellow mustaches, neglecting Raquel for the moment. "We haven't got any army, or any soldiers or officers or, . . . what the hell! With us everyone does as he damned well pleases. A lot of galley slaves, that's what we've got! And so, dearly beloved brethren, as a pal of mine used to say, 'Let's eat, drink, and be merry, for tomorrow we run!' "

Obeying his own suggestion, to the general satisfaction of the company, the major produced a bottle and passed it round. Raquel made a face, pretended to hesitate, and sought Don Sinforoso's eye.

"Go ahead. Take it," he said in her ear. "It's all right. These are all respectable people."

Aurora, who, as soon as she was inside, had decided that the schoolmaster was a bore, failed to ask his permission as she touched glasses with the young officer.

The talk grew extraordinarily animated. Those interested in love-making devoted themselves to it seriously. The rest let themselves be carried away by martial enthusiasm.

"Yes, sir! Their victory was only a stroke of luck. Why, I myself was cut off at Celaya by the Carranzistas and the poor fools didn't even know they had won!"

"The fact is that the Yaquis did it all. They're holy terrors! There were Yaquis in the brush, Yaquis behind walls, Yaquis in the ditches! The place was crawling with the bastards! I can still feel 'em in my pants!"

Each officer gave his own version of the defeat and was hotly disputed.

Señor Rubalcaba coughed repeatedly in the direction of Don Sinforoso. Raquel was all but sitting on the young officer's knees, but Don Sinforoso was deep in a technical account of the battle.

"To begin with, you must accept the fact that Villa and Angeles together are simply unbeatable. Villa's first error was not to have waited for Angeles. Then, a line of fire without support is a defeated line. . . ."

"There you go about that line again!" interrupted an officer with some heat. "Why, we attacked without the slightest notion of what we were about! Ridiculous! You send your men into action just as if you took a beehive and chucked it in the fire!"

Aurora was shamelessly rubbing her cheeks against the rough whiskers of the major. The schoolmaster helplessly prodded Don Sinforoso in the ribs.

"Now I'm going to explain to you the difference between a dislocation and a fracture. A dislocation usually takes place in three successive phases. . . ."

With the pride of an expert Don Sinforoso took pencil and paper to illustrate his point. Señor Rubalcaba was so desperate by this time that he resolved upon heroic measures and, extending one leg under the table he kicked Don Sinforoso violently in the shins.

The colonel looked up startled and took in the situation at a glance. He stood up, saying that his train was due to leave, thanked his friends graciously, and shook hands all round.

"How much do I owe you, lad?"

This set off an immediate and general riot, as everyone hastened to empty his pockets of Villa money.

The two gallants offered their arms to the auxiliaries and were the first to go out and promenade on the station platform.

One by one the trains pulled out, faster and faster. A mud-colored soldier stood up on top of a car and blew assembly on a battered bugle. Below, the troops stirred. From the few booths still standing in the marketplace men ran out with rifles in their hands or slung over their backs, their mouths full of tortillas, some with an arm in a sling, or dirty rags wrapped round their heads, or one leg in splints. Many were unwounded; all were dejected. They scrambled up the iron steps of the cars and joined their women who had climbed like monkeys and were now returning with interest the obscenities of the soldiers on the ground. One woman was whimpering that she had lost her baby. A soldier went to her aid. Below, a woman in a rich fur coat, which gave her the appearance of a bear in a circus, tied a shawl under the little fellow's arms, which stuck out as he was hoisted up, while he indifferently licked the frijoles off the corners of his mouth.

The engine whistled, puffed blackly. Iron and wood creaked in protest and the train was off.

The officers worked a miracle and produced another bottle of brandy. The auxiliaries, of course, refused (Don Sinforoso and Señor Rubalcaba were hardhearted brutes!), but with petting and coaxing they soon gave in and the bottle was finished in two rounds.

"I've just thought of something," said the young officer. "Why don't we go for a ride in Irapuato?"

"A brilliant idea!" replied the major. "Permit me to embrace you!"

The auxiliaries clapped their hands, ignoring the plain and vigorous disapproval of Don Sinforoso and the schoolmaster.

"We've got two cars at our disposal. Naturally, we'll all go together."

"Impossible! We'll miss our train."

"We'll be back in half an hour."

The auxiliaries were dying to go. Their eyes were shining, their gestures eloquent. They threw themselves on Don Sinforoso's neck. Their tender little nickerings would have moved a heart of stone.

The young officer, meanwhile, ran out and called the two chauffeurs. He stood talking animatedly to one of them. The chauffeur seemed to get the point, smiled and nodded.

Don Sinforoso and Señor Rubalcaba were escorted

to one of the cars and, overwhelmed with kindness, had to accept. Whereupon the two officers went back for the girls and the four of them leaped lightly into the first car. Sirens wailed, the way was cleared, and they disappeared in a dusty whirlwind.

Bang! The second car stopped abruptly. The chauffeur jumped down. A blowout! Don Sinforoso and Señor Rubalcaba had a feeling that all was not well. They changed color and avoided each other's eyes.

"Caramba!"

It was bad. The chauffeur scratched one ear.

"Can't go on. The tire's busted and the other guy's got all the tools. We can't fix it till they get back."

The first car was out of sight behind a curtain of dust. Its siren screamed insults.

XI EXPONENT OF ENERGY

In the shadow of a half-demolished shanty near the tarry oil tanks, Colonel Sinforoso, Señor Rubalcaba, and the two Zamora majors stopped to hold a council of war. Don Sinforoso's voice was hoarse and dull; he spoke in monosyllables; his face was tragic. His subject was the terrible defeat of Villa's party. With the sound of his own words Don Sinforoso was trying to drown the memory of the dear dream that he had lost.

The schoolmaster had no heart for evasions or vain resistance. His spirit was absent and his eyes were fixed on the white ribbon of road down which the car bearing his Aurora had disappeared. Alas, Aurora, Miss Aurora of the fourth grade! What was there about her? Something hers alone, something as intimate as her scarlet cap with the gold spangles, as intimate as her purple silk slippers stitched with silver thread, as intimate as the cool leather chair in which Señor Rubalcaba took his siesta in the mild May afternoons. He could hear the high, even voice of his Aurora: "Come, children! Hands in place! One, two, three! First position. . . . Where are your hands, Roberto? As we were saying yesterday . . . What were we saying yesterday? Who can tell me what we were saying yesterday? Hands!"

Ah, it is not as easy to cast off the habit of five years as it is to take off one's shirt upon going to bed, still less if it is a sweet and comfortable habit, and very much less if one is forty-eight, has a potbelly and an occasional attack of gout!

The schoolmaster's lips were fashioned for irony rather than pain, but they were learning a new expression now. His lascivious eyes were dull because they no longer reflected the light they once received.

Colonel Sinforoso was holding forth in the midst of a respectful silence when Moralitos approached and said in his cavernous voice: "What, gentlemen? You still here?"

Thick drops of sweat furrowed his dust-caked cheeks. Faces brightened for a moment. Handshakings, embraces, cordial greetings.

Meanwhile, like a pot coming to a boil, a tempest was brewing silently in Señor Rubalcaba's breast.

Sighs struggling to the surface made his double chin tremble but they were lost in the wheezing of his asthmatic lungs.

Señor Ríos, covered with dirt, his hair plastered to his forehead, cheeks, and ears, followed behind Moralitos His mustaches hung like limp mouse tails. After him came Don Rodolfo, perfectly calm and still wearing his beatific smile. Bringing up the rear, as always, was Neftalí, white with dust, his hat crushed, his shoes untied, the loose sole of one of them opening and closing like the jaw of a crocodile.

The latest rumors were passed around. Don Rodolfo agreed that they were very bad.

"What are you saying?" shouted Don Sinforoso, seizing Don Rodolfo's sleeve and pulling him face to face. "Those are not rumors, my friend! Those are facts, absolute facts! I'm an ex-federal and I know what I'm talking about!"

His glance was threatening, his smile terrible.

"I know the whole story. Villa is done for, annihilated!"

"Totally!" sobbed Señor Ríos and subsided, unable to continue.

"But," interposed Don Rodolfo, "we do have something left, something truly important, something that will save us. Believe me, gentlemen, we have something a bit better."

Don Rodolfo felt a hot breath in his ear.

"Now it's the turn of you pacifists. Ciudad Juárez taken! General Huerta and Pascual Orozco at Chihuahua! Félix Díaz in Oaxaca! It will take only three weeks more, believe me, my friend! And then? And then?"

Don Sinforoso's eyes shone like an owl's at midnight.

"The truth of the matter is, my military friends," said Moralitos, "that the Carranzistas are right on your heels."

"Right on our heels? Right on whose heels?"

Don Sinforoso spoke slowly and distinctly. He was in a tearing rage.

"My dear colonel, I only meant that you military gentlemen are in grave danger at this very moment. The rest of us, after all, are only humble government clerks who have nothing to do with politics or fighting."

"Exactly so!" chimed in Señor Ríos, vastly interested. "We are honest, peaceful, inoffensive citizens who have spent our lives within the four walls of an office. Our only crime is that we offered our services to anyone who demanded them, in exchange for our daily bread."

"Naturally!" added Moralitos. "We aren't mixed up in politics or parties. We are only defending what is ours, our jobs. Our common interest is food."

The solid arguments of Señor Ríos and Moralitos put a seal on Don Sinforoso's lips. The rest were worried. The schoolmaster alone was indifferent, his eyes still fixed on the highway, hoping for a miracle.

Don Rodolfo spoke, his eternal smile on his face.

"Gentlemen, I'm delighted that your spirits see some feeble hint of the light that will guide us out of the darkness in which we are living. Half an hour ago I caught a glimpse of that light myself, but I doubted my own eyes, and in the general excitement I didn't dare mention my discovery. Now I can do so without the slightest hesitation. What good, I have been asking myself, what good are we doing for ourselves in following these men who have already stepped over the brink of the precipice?"

Señor Ríos stared at Don Rodolfo, stupefied, his face pasty with anguish.

"Why, we've got to save ourselves from the clutches of those murderers!"

Don Rodolfo patted him gently on the shoulder and turned to Neftalí.

"Don't you think, Neftalí, that since we are complete strangers in Irapuato we could await events here. The Carranzistas will take us for citizens of the town and the townspeople will take us for Carranzistas."

Neftalí was lying doubled up against the side of the hut, fagged out, disconsolately surveying the disaster to his shoes. He answered Don Rodolfo with a grimace which, interpreted, meant: "You are quite aware that I live in my ivory tower, that my spirit floats serenely above the eternal snows, indifferent to these trifles you call revolution."

"The fact is," said Moralitos, "that the stories we hear about General Obregón aren't at all discouraging for us. They say he not only guarantees the safety of noncombatants, but even passes out a little money to peaceable and honest citizens."

His hearers licked their lips, all but Señor Ríos. He felt himself alone, immensely alone, his gaze lost in the sadness of the white earth and the smoke of the trains.

Don Sinforoso meditated, scowling. One of the Zamora majors, the notary, discreetly disappeared behind the hut, removed his leggings and hid them, together with his rifle, under a pile of rotten wood and rubbish. When he returned, no one noticed the change.

They set off in silence down a narrow road toward a thick clump of trees, where the earth was green from the dripping of a water pipe.

Don Rodolfo took Señor Ríos to one side.

"To be or not to be, friend. Are you staying?"

"I'd rather die, Don Rodolfo!"

"Well, I'm staying."

He was silent for a moment.

"Señor Ríos, our companionship, the bond of our profession, and the very particular affection I feel for you, oblige me to offer you everything I have against a day that is almost upon us. I am staying here and I know what I'm about. I have friends and colleagues high in Señor Carranza's government. I repeat, they need us. If they succeed we shall be more necessary to them than their rifles are now. I wish, my dear friend, you could see things more calmly."

"Never! Impossible! What? Work for them? Never!" whispered Señor Ríos lugubriously.

"I'm sorry, but don't you see that our old department heads are, perhaps, the only ones who have really lost out, which leaves a career for the rest of us that we never dreamed of! The day you realize clearly the opportunity I am offering you, you will bless the revolution, as I do now, for the good it is bringing us."

"Please, Don Rodolfo! I shouldn't believe it if I weren't hearing it with my own ears!"

"Try and understand me, Señor Ríos. We have in

our hands the most unexpected, the most unbelievable triumph. When the pie that those gentlemen had prepared (forgive my coarse figure!) was baked and each caudillo seized his piece, we fell upon our portion with the appetite of flypaper on a hot day. How did the caudillos feel about that? Why, they felt themselves most honored by the distinction, trust, and affection we gave them in their hour of need, and they gave us the nod. Once we had to bear the odium of being called Huertistas or Felixistas, and today they pompously say we are disloyal. But we on this side of the fence are just as loyal as those on the other. And so, Señor Ríos, if we have thus far firmly and stoically succeeded in maintaining our position in or out of office, why should we retreat in the very moment of our trial, now that we are about to reveal ourselves to the world as authentic exponents of energy?"

Señor Ríos made a face as if he had just swallowed a large dose of quinine.

"What a shameful thing it is for us," proceeded Don Rodolfo, "to think that many of our former inferiors have achieved the very limit of their aspirations!"

"My single aspiration," replied Señor Ríos, unyielding, "is to put the sea between that scum and me!"

"In any case, and whatever you decide to do, I want you to know that I . . . unconditionally. . . ."

"The Carranzistas! The Carranzistas!"

At Moralitos' shrill screams all scattered and hid themselves behind the posts of the oil tank. In his mad haste Neftalí Sancho Peredo de la Garza tripped over his broken shoe and left an imprint of his handsome face in the mud. Only Don Rodolfo preserved his enviable calm and went to investigate.

People were running about in all directions. The noise swelled like an angry sea. Sharp cries could be heard above the rumble of the crowd, shots here and there.

"For sweet Jesus' sake, gentlemen!" implored Moralitos. "You officers must not stay here and compromise us! I beg you, by Our Lady of Guadalupe, go away quickly! If those devils catch us here with you they will kill us too!"

"Calm yourself, my friend," said Don Sinforoso, with stoic fortitude. "I'm not an officer. Look, here in my wallet is my commission as chief of police of my home town since before the revolution. I've never been anything else. Just as much a civilian as the rest of you."

The Zamora tailor, pale as wax, turned to his friend the notary and was dumbfounded at his transformation—no arms or any military insignia. His mouth was so dry that his words stuck to his tongue.

"I'm not an officer either!" he yelled. "Certainly not! What the devil! I'm only a poor little unlucky tailor from Zamora, that's all!"

So saying, he gave such a furious yank at the star on his hat that he tore off a piece of felt with it, and threw his rifle into a water hole, where it sunk with a dull plop.

Meanwhile, the crowd had become quiet again. Rumor had it that the row was started by the Villistas themselves who had been chasing a thief and shot him behind the freight shed.

A train puffed into the station.

"I'm off!" shouted Señor Ríos, suddenly inspired, as he made a dash for the station platform.

Moralitos, obeying the inexorable force of destiny, took off after him. Don Sinforoso and Señor Rubalcaba exchanged perplexed glances and searched the road down which their faithless ones had vanished. They questioned each other mutely, lifted their eyes in resignation, and set out after Moralitos as fast as they could run. Only Don Rodolfo and Neftalí remained.

"Señor Ríos! Señor Ríos! You've forgotten your things, Señor Ríos!"

"Never mind, Neftalí. He can't hear you. That's not the only thing they forgot. Moralitos forgot his grandmother!"

A few moments later, when the train had gone and the last car had disappeared, Don Rodolfo bent over and picked up Señor Ríos' Russia leather bag and his new English topcoat. He invited Neftalí to collect the rifles, leggings, and the rest of their friends' belongings. They got a porter to help them carry the heavy load to a streetcar.

"Just an advance on our salary, Neftalí," said Don Rodolfo, smiling with Franciscan benevolence.

XII VILLA PAPER

The rails were clear only the few moments between the departure of one train and the arrival of the next. With every brigade that left, the same clanging and bustle. The trains pulled out one after the other. The troops collapsed in heaps wherever they could find a free spot. Some, completely used up, fell asleep where they dropped. On the roofs miniature encampments appeared, made by hanging blankets over clothes lines strung between stacked rifles.

Marta and her children, followed by Señor Quiñones, got off a streetcar. Marta was carrying half a dozen chickens tied by their feet. Their bloodshot heads were raised, their beaks dripped, and their little round eyes were the color of yellow porcelain. Rubén had the bag of provisions and Matilde and Quiñones the luggage. They were looking for General Malacara.

"It's true, isn't it, Quiñones, that Rubén will be all right if he stays with you?" asked Marta, her eyes puffy from weeping.

"I know Obregón quite well . . . practically friends."

"He's an intimate friend of Obregón!" said Marta, turning to Rosita.

Although Quiñones was only a schoolmate of Rubén, from that moment he assumed gigantic proportions. Rubén patted him on the back; Rosita displayed her charms; Matilde smiled at him like a loving sister. Marta left off calling him "Quiñones" and gave him the new title of "Señor Quiñones".

They made their way to the station platform. Marta beckoned to Matilde.

"If Rubén stays behind, I stay too."

"But, Mama, that's nonsense! In that case we'd all have to stay. Why did we leave home in the first place? We've got a pass to Ciudad Juárez, General Malacara's 5000 pesos and General Villa's 10,000."

"But if anything should happen to Rubén?"

"Have you lost your wits? Didn't you hear Quiñones say he's an intimate friend of Obregón? With Quiñones on our side we'll get everything we want. Rubén will stay here and get jobs for us. We'll go on as far as León or Aguascalientes, where we'll sell our passes and change our money. If things break for Villa we'll wait for Rubén there. If he keeps on losing we'll come back when the danger is over, a matter of two weeks or less."

"Señor Quiñones," asked Marta stubbornly, "couldn't we get silver for some of our paper?"

"Villa paper? Ha, ha, ha!"

"Mama, for goodness' sake, don't be silly!"

"But we bought all this stuff with Villa money."

"Maybe somebody will take it," said Quiñones. "I've got a notion to paper my house with it. It would be cheaper than wallpaper."

"Hush, Señor Quiñones! I think someone's listening."

Rubén indicated one of the dorados of General Villa's bodyguard.

Their attention was diverted by shouting and a fresh commotion. Another train was pulling out. People heaped up in the cars and on the roofs. Hammocks slung between truss rods, with fat women bouncing in them like fish caught in a net. Naked children. Soldiers, red-eyed and filthy. Withered faces gathered at the doors. Slowly the cars rolled past. A little altar went by, decorated with wild roses and pictures of the Virgin. From a window hung a cage with a lark in it. In another a broken crock did duty as a flower pot. Confused heaps of hairy heads, brown ponchos, greasy clothing, shining machetes, the polished brass of band instruments. Moving faster now, a carload of horses passed, their nostrils dilated. Through the bars their black eyes contemplated curiously the milling mob below them. Faster and faster the interminable rosary of cars sped by and disappeared at last, leaving upon the retina the image of roofs covered with moving heads, gleaming rifles, blankets and ponchos bellying in the wind.

"*The swallows will return again*," hummed Quiñones mockingly. "Whatever," he asked Matilde in astonishment, "whatever gave you the notion of joining up with that rabble?"

"Necessity, Señor Quiñones. Why, you yourself. . . . Aren't you working for them?"

"I work for them, but I don't tag along with them —which is a very different kind of thing."

"God knows, Señor Quiñones, we didn't come here because we wanted to!" said Marta in anguish. "Why, the Carranzistas even threatened to kill us!"

"We know what *they* are like!" added Matilde. "It was enough to break your heart yesterday when we left. They sacked the stores and stuffed their trains with goods. What they couldn't carry off they gave to the people! Bandits!"

"Oh, the Carranzistas aren't really like that, Matilde. You'll see how nice, how polite, how courteous, the Obregón men can be."

Eloquence was not precisely Quiñones' forte, but he pronounced a panegyric on the First Chief with such feeling that Rubén took fright, seeing the dorado making straight for them.

"Watch out, Quiñones! He's listening!"

"Oh, there's nothing to fear from those dogs now. General Obregón pulled their teeth at Celaya. The dorados! Jackals of that bandit Arango!"

But his last words froze in his throat and his heart sank into his boots as the dorado accosted them.

"So you're buying up Villa money to paper your house? Just come along with me and I'll sell you some."

"I, sir?" cried the terrified Rubén. "I never said such a thing in my life!"

His protests were in vain and his jaw sagged as the dorado grabbed him.

Marta let out a scream and dropped her chickens. Rosita caught her as she fainted.

"Leave my brother alone, you tramp!" cried Matilde. "Don't you know who we are? Let him go, you scoundrel! We're the Reyes-Téllez of Culiacán! You hear me, you low scum? Let my brother go!"

The dorado pushed Matilde roughly to one side and dragged Rubén away. Matilde turned into a she cat. She threw herself at the dorado, seized him by the coat, tore off buttons, made ribbons of one sleeve, scratched his face and pulled his hair.

"Stop it, you bitch!"

Rosita, with her mother in her arms, was unable to come to Matilde's help. The uproar grew. Matilde shrieked. A crowd gathered. Officers appeared. Rubén was almost unconscious.

Rosita finally managed to lean her mother against a tree and began furiously to open bags and bundles, prodding and turning everything inside out. She turned imploring eyes in all directions. Her anguish grew as Matilde and Rubén disappeared in the crowd. She could still hear Matilde's high-pitched curses. however, when an officer approached.

"What's the matter with the lady?"

"She fainted when they arrested my brother. But I swear he's innocent, sir! See here!"

She unfolded under the officer's nose some papers she had found in an old shoe, stowed away among hairbrushes and dirty clothes.

"Oh, sir, if you would be so good! Make them let him go!"

The officer called a soldier and put him in charge of Marta and the luggage. He offered his arm to Rosita, but she pulled her tight skirt above her knees and ran off to join Matilde and Rubén.

"Señor Dorado, you've made a mistake! We're Villistas! See here! Here's a pass that General Villa himself just gave me! Let my brother go, Señor Dorado! I give you my word that he didn't say anything."

Rosita found the patience necessary to convince the dorado that Rubén was not a Carranzista after all.

"In fact," added the officer, "these young ladies are government employees, and this young man is also."

"Yes, but this bird here said he was buying up General Villa's money to paper his house, and I'm going to give him enough to paper even the mother that gave him birth."

"No, sir. We were only trying to sell a few bills, because we know you can't buy anything in the stations up ahead except with silver."

"Well, then, where's that other bird?"

"There he goes!" exclaimed Rubén, who had come

to. "See! There he goes, running across the bridge!"

With huge delight he pointed to Quiñones, who was flying over the streetcar bridge as if the devil were after him.

"Well, by the mother . . . ! I'll get him if it's the last act of my life! Look here, friend, I'll let you off, but you've got to tell me who the guy is. Give me his name and address and I'll get him, no matter where he hides out!"

Rubén would have spilled everything he knew, but Matilde stopped him.

"Shut up! . . . Sir, this is what happened. We were in the streetcar and we asked if someone wouldn't change our money for banknotes or silver, and that gentleman who ran away said he would if we'd pay him a big premium. But he didn't mean a word of it. All he wanted was to make a date."

"Let's get out of this accursed town as fast as we can!" were Marta's first words.

She asked for Rubén, and looked him over and touched him until she convinced herself that her senses were not deceiving her, and covered him with kisses.

Rosita and Matilde picked up the luggage, which was considerably lighter.

"Matilde, what became of the chickens?"

Matilde was about to ask the officer about them, but Marta opposed her stoutly. Her single thought was to take the first train out. So they set off in search of General Malacara, who had promised them a place in the governor's car.

XIII A MOTHER'S HEROISM

No one knew anything about General Malacara's train. The station master was sitting at a desk turning over mountains of paper: white, blue, yellow, all colors. After keeping Marta and her brood waiting for half an hour, he took pity on them. The train dispatcher, he said, was the only one who could tell them. For twenty pesos, paper, an urchin guided them to the dispatcher's car. That gentleman, whose face suggested a carnival mask, was solemnly and blankly staring at a piece of blue paper covered with white curlicues. At the end of twenty minutes he condescended to speak.

"You were saying . . . ?"

He fell silent again. Ten minutes passed while he continued his scrutiny of the blue paper.

"Oh yes. . . . General Malacara. . . . Hum. . . . Young ladies, General Malacara's train left here at eight this morning."

"Excuse me, sir, but that can't be true. It happens that we were with him when he got here at ten."

But the dispatcher had lost himself again in his papers. Matilde restrained a violent urge to pull his whiskers.

"You were inquiring . . . ?" he said at last, as the family was going out the door.

"About General Malacara. . . . Please, sir!"

"Oh yes. General Malacara, General Malacara. . . .

I'm sorry, my young friends, but there's no general of that name in the Northern Division."

"But," explained Rubén patiently, "we told you that we came here with him this morning."

The dispatcher studied his map.

"Well, my young friends, he must have deceived you!"

The Reyes-Téllez rushed out in a fury just as a train was passing. They recognized the hospital car. At the door, their legs dangling, sat the doctor and the major.

Marta and her children ran shouting with joy. The train happened to stop and they scrambled on board.

"The doctor! The doctor!"

"It's our dear little doctor!"

"What luck!" exclaimed Marta, beaming.

"Isn't this nice!" cried Rosita, enveloping the doctor in a glance of gratitude and tenderness.

A leathery smile wrinkled the doctor's face.

"Oh doctor, you knew we'd look you up, didn't you? One is either a friend or one isn't. What did you think of us! When we're friends we're friends for keeps!"

"That's right! We Reyes-Téllez are like that. Friends till death!"

They were still puffing from their run.

"Those others insisted on our going with them this morning, but we said: 'Never! What! Leave the company of our dear friend the doctor? We started out with him and we're going to stick with him!' "

"Only we've got to leave Rubén behind, doctor. He's had a stomach upset and he'd better stay here in Irapuato."

Marta could hardly believe her ears. Rubén's face

grew long and yellow as a melon. But Matilde talked so fast and gave them so little time to protest, eyeing them threateningly the while, that even Marta did not dare interrupt her.

"Rubén will be in no danger, doctor. He'll be perfectly safe in the home of a friend of ours. . . . Oh, doctor, you can't imagine what a time we had finding your car!"

"By the way, doctor," asked Rosita, sweet as sugar, "what car is General Malacara in?"

"General Malacara played a fine trick on us," answered the doctor, grinning.

"Did he go in another train?"

"He left two hours ago, in the governor's train, with some very pretty company."

Matilde turned livid. Rosita caught her breath. The doctor left them coolly and rejoined the major at the door.

The engine whistled and the train began to move. Marta and her family installed themselves in the dark interior of the now deserted car. Matilde led Rubén to the door. He protested, but she seized his arm and propelled him vigorously.

"You're going to get off and hide among the houses until it gets dark. Then you're going to find Quiñones. No one will recognize you in the dark, not even the dorado."

"Matilde, for God's sake!" implored Marta.

Matilde drew herself up and folded her arms.

"Stop it! After being robbed this afternoon do you want us to lose everything else as well? Do you really want Rubén to go with us, no matter what? Very well, then, let him come!"

At which Matilde opened her blouse, extracted a thick bundle of bills and the passes to Ciudad Juárez and solemnly made as if to throw them out the door.

Marta's hand, skinny and dry as an eagle's claw, stopped her.

"No, Matilde!"

"Well, then?"

Marta bowed her head and closed her eyes.

"Good-bye, my boy! In the name of the Father, Son, and Holy Ghost!"

"Amen!" answered Rubén reverently, dropping on one knee, kissing Marta's hand and lowering his head.

The train slowed down at a switch. Matilde gently pushed her brother and he slipped past the doctor to the ground. The engine puffed and the train was soon running at top speed.

XIV   CURTAIN

Little by little the station was emptied of trains, soldiers, and civilians. It was getting late. On the platforms no one remained but the dorados pacing back and forth. Thinning groups of people watched the end of the evacuation.

General Villa's polished locomotive was panting on a siding. On the boiler, just forward of the bell, a huge bronze eagle perched. A shield with the national tricolor glinted under the headlight. The engine drew only a single yellow box car, newly painted, and a Pullman.

The rear door of the Pullman opened. A thickset man in his shirtsleeves, a man with square, broad shoulders, ruddy face, and eyes that glowed like coals under heavy lids, stepped out on the vestibule. His watchful glance missed nothing. His great lion's head with its crisp hair was indomitably erect. His movements were slow and undulating, panther-like.

Absolute silence reigned about him. No mad clapping now, no wild cheers.

The whistle blew. The dorados sprinted for the cars. The man with the square shoulders and deadly feline eyes stepped backward without turning his head. His gaze was lost in the distance, where a white cloud of dust showed that the cavalry was covering his retreat. The cloud was shot through with a golden lacework, brush strokes drawn in hot gold by the dying sun, dying forever.

From across the warm breath of night came a distant, low, mysterious murmur, a murmur as solemn as the voice of the sea: "Mexico is saved!" And on the eastern horizon the white-faced, cross-eyed moon, laughing, laughing. . . .

THE BOSSES

CONTENTS

PART ONE, THE OLD RÉGIME   *93*

PART TWO, THE RIFT   *134*

PART THREE, DIES IRAE   *175*

LIST OF CHARACTERS

SETTING: *a small city in western Mexico, 1911–1913.*

THE DEL LLANO FAMILY *(the "caciques"), consisting of:*

    DON BERNABÉ, *the eldest brother;*

    DON IGNACIO, *the second brother, manager of the firm of Del Llano Bros., Inc.;*

    FATHER JEREMIAH, *the youngest brother;*

    TERESA, *the sister.*

LARA ROJAS AND VILLEGAS, *clerks at Del Llano Bros., Inc.*

JUAN VIÑAS, *a grocer, proprietor of* La Sultana;

    ELENA, *his wife;*

    ESPERANZA, *his daughter;*

    JUANITO, *his son.*

RODRÍGUEZ, *a clerk at* La Continental.

MEMBERS *of the Twentieth of November Club:*

    TIMOTEO OLIVA, *proprietor of* La Bandera Mexicana;

    CRISPÍN, *a news vendor;*

    FELÍCITOS GALLARDO, *the town orator;*

    PORFIRIO LÓPEZ, *called "the Pig."*

PART ONE

THE OLD RÉGIME

CHAPTER I

"It's Don Ignacio!" whispered a voice at the church door.

"It's Don Ignacio!" a hundred lips repeated. The people packed themselves together still more tightly to make room for the newcomer. Heads turned and eyes sought him anxiously, but Don Ignacio marched down the middle of the aisle, stern, inflexible, thin, his gaze fixed on the bier at the far end, on the silks, cords, tassels, ornaments, nickel plate, on the black coffin that displayed in great shining letters the initials of Don Juan José del Llano, founder of the respectable house of Del Llano & Sons, Inc.

The crowd was denser toward the bier, and it was only by pushing and elbowing that Don Ignacio was able to reach the railing, with its tall yellow candles and its row of prostrate mourners praying in silence.

Don Ignacio took out his handkerchief, spread it carefully on the dusty, worn carpet, and knelt, sweating and puffing.

"Lord, it's hot!" he muttered.

Don Bernabé, the eldest brother, turned his head. From a withered face a pair of burning old eyes peered out at him through a black shawl. An elegant lady, wearing a studied expression of deep grief, saluted him. Everyone was aware of the presence of Don Ignacio, the most important member of the Succession. Only Father Jeremiah, the youngest brother, standing at the left of the officiating priest, maintained his ecstatic pose, his eyes fixed upon the ceiling of the apse and the gilded splendor of the Holy Trinity. His emaciated armadillo's head hardly showed above the stiff brocade of his vestments.

"Thank you, Don Juan!" said Don Ignacio to a grimy, bent, and long-legged individual who offered him a candle.

On Don Juan's face, grateful for the "thank you," appeared the hint of a stolid smile as he stepped backward and mingled with the crowd, distributing his armful of candles right and left.

"Let me hold your hat, Nachito," said an old woman gently, devouring him with her eyes as she held out her skinny brown hand.

"Thank you!" said Don Ignacio.

"Nacho, I'm sorry, but I have to go. Awfully sorry, but it's nine o'clock and I left Dolores alone at the store. Your grief is my own, as you know. After all, we were schoolmates."

"Thank you, Don Timoteo!" answered Don Ignacio, addressing a man who dripped with perspiration and allowing his hand to be squeezed by the wet fingers of his ex-schoolmate.

"Don Ignacio! The second candle to your right—it might burn the altar boy."

Don Ignacio plucked the altar boy by the sleeve and motioned toward the candle. He turned.

"Thank you!" he said, unperturbed.

Everyone during the service sought a pretext to speak to Don Ignacio and express respect and loyalty for the great house of Del Llano & Sons, Inc., and Don Ignacio repeated his tireless "thank you" until the priests, one behind the other, made their last march three times round the bier to drive the devil away.

The ceremony ended. Six husky peasants raised the bright new coffin to their shoulders and carried it out, followed by all the mourners.

The day was magnificent. Torrents of sunlight inundated the city and the golden hills surrounding it. The crowd dispersed in all directions and only the black frock coats accompanied Don Juan José del Llano to his last resting place.

CHAPTER II

"What are you telling me? Corn at five-fifty? You're joking, Villegas. Why, you yourself are selling it at five-thirty!"

Lara Rojas stretched his bovine neck as if his stiff shirt were bothering him, looked sharply at the angelically stupid face of Don Juan Viñas and stifled a laugh.

"Don Juan," he said, "I'll pay you twelve pesos a hectoliter for all the corn you can buy a week from now at six pesos."

Don Juan wanted to take him up, but Villegas, a short, fat, very red little man, stopped the argument.

"Hush, gentlemen! More respect, please!"

He took Lara Rojas by the arm and led him off ahead of the procession.

"You mustn't say such things to Don Juan, Lara Rojas. You'll never make him understand."

"But you can't make me believe that Juan Viñas, a man who has made a fortune selling beans and rice, doesn't know about such things," scoffed Lara Rojas.

He was about to burst into one of his noisy laughs when he noticed the proximity of the coffin and the solemn faces of the mourners, and his laughter, as if by magic, became a deep, sincere, and heart-felt sigh.

Don Bernabé del Llano turned his gray head and fixed his tired chicken's gaze on Lara Rojas, who congratulated himself on having been able to sigh so opportunely. Lara Rojas' eyes were lamb-like in their gentleness and he almost managed to squeeze out a tear or two.

The procession halted. The tired pallbearers yielded to their alternates. The eleven o'clock sun forced off hats and bald spots were furtively exposed. Ill humor appeared on some faces and many showed distinct signs of boredom.

A pair of bony donkeys, cropping parched grass in a stubble field, raised their heads and contemplated the funeral procession, which they scornfully dismissed with switching tails and wagging ears.

The procession started up again. Bringing up the rear were Juan Viñas and Rodríguez, clerk at *La Continental.*

"I tell you it can't be done!" insisted Viñas. "Villegas can't buy corn at five-fifty, because he himself has forced the market down to five-thirty."

"But, Don Juan," answered Rodríguez, "this is the very ABC of business. Try and understand. Villegas floods the market with corn at five-thirty. Very well, then, no seller can find anyone to buy it at its proper price of five-fifty except Villegas."

"That's exactly what I don't get."

"It's as clear as this sun that's frying us. Villegas sells a thousand hectoliters at five-thirty and buys ten thousand at five-fifty."

"And so . . . ?"

Rodríguez took out his handkerchief and mopped his damp forehead.

"And so? Well, when he has cornered all the grain, he waits a very short time and at the right moment he offers it on the market, fixing whatever price he pleases."

Don Juan opened his eyes very wide.

"But it's elementary, Don Juan!"

"Call it anything you like, friend Rodríguez, but, frankly, the business doesn't look clean to me. I don't know how to explain it to you. . . . What? An honorable house, like the Del Llanos. . . ."

"Those birds?"

"Yes, sir! An honorable house like Del Llano & Sons, Inc., doesn't do that kind of business."

It was Rodríguez' turn to open his eyes. Here was a rare specimen of grocer! He didn't know whether to laugh or groan. They were interrupted by a hoarse curse. The manager of *La Carolina* had stumbled and bumped one of his corns atrociously.

The procession threaded the last alleys of the city and came out on the highway lined with stone walls and hedges of prickly pears. The white enclosure of the cemetery glistened in the sun. Its spartan entrance was without an ornament, without a molding, without a single imperfection. Everything about it was pure and white, like a freshly whitewashed stable.

The last to throw a handful of earth into the grave was Don Juan Viñas. As he lugubriously took leave of the Del Llano brothers Don Ignacio took him by the arm in a friendly fashion and together they left the cemetery.

"The good are called from us," sighed Don Juan.

Silence. Don Juan, feeling the need of pronouncing a eulogy on the deceased, began again.

"The good. . . ."

"Are the final papers in order?" interrupted Don Ignacio.

Don Juan was taken aback and hesitated a moment.

"Everything has been done as you advised," he answered timidly. "You don't know, Don Ignacio, how infinitely grateful. . . ."

"How about the bricks and lime?"

"Six tons to begin with. They're baking the first batch of bricks down at the yard. The workmen have finished the grading. Today, of course, no one worked. We went to the services in a body. It was our duty. I passed the candles round myself. . . . I'll never be able to repay you. . . . Never!"

But Don Ignacio's face showed no interest in eulogies and Don Juan ended by talking business pure and simple. At every corner they were interrupted by mourners who took their leave of Don Ignacio.

"Do you know, Don Ignacio," said Don Juan, when his turn came, "I still have some uneasy moments at **night** about this project."

"No reason for it," replied Don Ignacio coldly. "I've shown you with figures how safe it is."

"True. I shall be eternally grateful to the Del Llanos, to your dead father. . . ."

Don Juan raised his handkerchief to his child-like eyes, from which great tears were rolling.

CHAPTER III

"Didn't you go to the cemetery, Don Timoteo?"

"Only to the services, Mariquita. After all, Don Ignacio was a schoolmate of mine, but now he treats me as if he'd never seen me. I come from the common herd; they are caciques. But they're heading for a fall one of these days!"

"How's the revolution going, Don Timoteo?"

"It's coming, child. It's here! We've won!"

"But they say the revolutionists are very bad men who kill and steal."

Don Timoteo got up from his armchair and removed his woolen skullcap. He passed his thick hand gently over his tomato-like cranium. He spoke slowly and his gaze lost itself in the dusty length of the street, where the electric lights were beginning to twinkle. The last band of sunlight vanished from the house tops. Fleecy clouds tumbled about in the topaz sky.

"Mariquita," said Don Timoteo, "the gentlemen of the firm you're working for call the revolutionists thieves and murderers. That's what the caciques call them. And they're right, Mariquita! The revolution is a matter of life and death to the caciques. Just as the clergy met their doom with Benito Juárez, the caciques are meeting theirs with Francisco Madero. . . . And before I forget it, Mariquita, tell the Del Llanos I've got some Comanja biscuit. Casianito is crazy about them. . . . Yes, the caciques are the plague that's destroying us!"

"What are caciques, Don Timoteo?"

"Did you hear that, Dolores? Mariquita doesn't know what caciques are! Don't I say a thousand times a day that the ignorance of the masses is a national calamity? The caciques, Mariquita, are . . . are . . . the worst people in the world. Very wicked men. Scoundrels, in fact. I can't explain it very well. I'll give you several numbers of *El País* to read so you can get an idea of what those rascals are like. Dolores, bring me my file of newspapers."

"Never mind, Don Timoteo. I read very badly and I haven't got the patience for all that. But there really aren't any of them in our part of the world, are there?"

"Oh, sweet innocence! What are you saying, Mariquita! Why, you're living with caciques! You're working for caciques! Your bosses are caciques!"

"Hum. Then those stories in your papers are nothing but exaggerations, Don Timoteo. Don't believe a word of it! As far as I am concerned there's nobody as good as little Casianito. Who do you think gave me these shoes?"

"Let me see, Mariquita."

"Timoteo!" cried Dolores from the back of the store.

She emerged bringing three pounds of rice for Mariquita.

As soon as the girl had left, Don Timoteo caressed his wife's round arms and patted her backside.

"You've got to plant the seed, Dolores," he said, "before you can gather in the crop. The ignorance of the masses is a national calamity! Anyone who doesn't fight ignorance is a criminal. The ignorance of the masses is the reason why we had to live under the heel of that dictator Porfirio Díaz for forty years!"

"Don't preach at me, Timoteo! What's all that got to do with Mariquita's shoes, old idiot?"

"Ouch! Don't pinch so hard, Dolores. I'm old. You do very well to remind me of it; and just because I *am* old I don't want to die without first sowing the seed of my doctrines. Man dies, Dolores; ideas live on. Ideas are imperishable, eternal!"

"Our souls are the only eternal things we've got, and that's what we should be looking after. Go in and get your coat, old muttonhead, and we'll go to Capuchinas for prayers."

"But today is the club meeting, Dolores!"

Dolores put Don Timoteo's coat on for him, locked up *La Bandera Mexicana,* and marched him off without saying another word.

"We must pay for the sins of our fathers as well as our own," lamented Don Timoteo. "You're right, Dolores. You are merely obeying your education, the education we Mexicans give our women. We take better care of our dogs and cats than we do of you!"

The pair entered the church. Their footsteps resounded in the cold darkness under the vaulted roof.

The pulpit could only be guessed at. A bored priest was mumbling through the rosary and a dozen beshawled women were repeating the responses in a feeble and monotonous whine. The purple robes of Our Lord Jesus of Calvary could be dimly made out in the light of the flickering oil lamp.

Don Timoteo began to associate ideas: "Christ, Redeemer of the world; Hidalgo, redeemer of the race; Juárez, redeemer of consciences; Madero, redeemer of the poor and humble."

Don Timoteo trembled with emotion. What a subject for a speech at the club!

"Our Father, who art in heaven, hallowed be Thy name; Thy kingdom come. . . ." droned the priest.

Overcome by his feelings, Don Timoteo fell to his knees and prayed rapidly: "Thy kingdom come, the kingdom of just honest men, and death to the dirty *cientificos!** The kingdom of men of good will, the kingdom of the gentle-hearted, of those who hunger and thirst after justice, as Don Justo Sierra said."

Don Timoteo rose and left the church precipitately.

At the club he was in great form. He compared Juárez and Madero with Christ, repeating that "respect for our neighbor's rights is peace," and that "we should give unto God that which is God's and unto Caesar that which is Caesar's." And finally he gave his word of honor that there had never been a better defender of religion than Benito Juárez and that the clergy ought to erect a monument to him.

---

* The *cientificos* (scientists) were President Díaz' economic and political cabinet, headed by José Limantour, Minister of the Treasury.

The most eminent members of the club looked at each other in amazement.

"I didn't think he had it in him," remarked the vice-president, who was also second trombone in the municipal band.

Crispín, who sold newspapers and had no breeding, broke the spell.

"What a memory you've got, Don Timoteo! You've learned by heart every single word of the editorial in *El Diario del Hogar!*"

"Bless my soul! You're right, Crispín!" exclaimed Don Timoteo, clapping a hand to his forehead and scaring off the mosquitoes. "It's a fact! What I said *was* in today's paper, but I swear I didn't remember it and thought the idea came to me just a while ago, while I was at prayers in Capuchinas. Anyway, the notion about the monument to Juárez was mine and nobody else's."

Relieved of an enormous weight, Don Timoteo returned to the church to finish his prayers, which he said with great devotion, at the same time computing a bill for fifty tins of lard he had shipped to Torreón that afternoon.

CHAPTER IV

As Don Juan Viñas was returning from the brickyard that evening on his way to the Del Llanos', he stopped in at *La Bandera Mexicana.*

"Don Timoteo, let's go and express our sympathy to the Del Llanos."

"I hadn't even thought of it, Don Juan."

"But, man, it's the Del Llanos! Who doesn't owe favors to the Del Llanos?"

Don Timoteo shrugged his shoulders.

"Bah! Favors! However, I'll go. After all, Don Ignacio and I were schoolmates. Only when you're poor, Don Juan, you're kind of ashamed."

Don Juan took him by the arm and led him off.

Not until they were on the doorstep did Don Juan notice that his shoes were spotted with lime and mud and that he was in his working clothes. But he wiped his shoes on the back of his legs, beat the collar and lapels of his coat and the front of his trousers with great violence, and felt more or less presentable. Dazzled by the light inside, he failed to recognize the mourners in black who filled the corridor. He approached one of them.

"Please, can you tell me . . . ? The señores . . . ?"

"Oh, it's Don Juan! The señores? This way."

Lara Rojas took Don Juan's arm and pushed him suddenly into the middle of a room full of women. Taken by surprise, Don Juan stood tongue-tied, his hands in his pockets, while Lara Rojas hurried out smothering his laughter. Don Juan retreated in embarrassment, just as Don Ignacio, Don Bernabé, and Father Jeremiah emerged from the study to send the parish priest on his way.

Friends of the family hastened to salute Don Ignacio, who greeted Don Juan most cordially, threw an arm over his shoulders and led him into the study.

Lara Rojas bit his lip. Don Timoteo, who had been

glued to a post in the corridor, seized the opportunity to escape to the street, philosophizing on the vanity and insolence of caciques.

"Did you notice, Villegas," said Lara Rojas, when they were out of the house, "did you notice how intimate that clown of a Don Juan is with Don Ignacio? What do you make of it?"

Villegas moved his restless little eyes, sucked hard on his penny cigar, and shrugged. The cashier of the National Bank answered for him.

"There's no mystery about it. Don Juan Viñas, with the backing of the Del Llanos, is building a big model village for workingmen."

"Don Juan Viñas?" asked Lara Rojas scornfully.

"Don Juan Viñas, my boy, has got forty thousand pesos in cash! And this is the same Juan Viñas who came here in leather pants, yellow brogans, and a rough straw hat, the Juan Viñas who built a shed out of several dozen adobes, a heap of straw, and a few loads of thatch, and who then set up shop in it with some ill-assorted bottles filled with colored water. And this is the same Juan Viñas who today owns the best grocery store in town!"

Rodríguez, who was always spoiling for an argument, broke into the conversation.

"I wonder, gentlemen, if you realize the privations, the sleepless nights, and the endless economies that those forty thousand pesos represent."

"I shouldn't want to get rich at that price," said Lara Rojas disdainfully.

"A fortune of forty thousand pesos," continued Rodríguez, "won by twenty years of hard work, when a man is young, may possibly be the fortune of an

honest man—that is, as far as it's possible for a merchant to be honest—because, my friends, you can't
convince me that you can come into this world without even a bandage for your belly and pile up a fortune of half a million pesos honestly, no matter how
long you live."

"I don't know who you're talking about," retorted
Villegas, irritated. He tossed away his cigar angrily
and continued: "If you're talking about the Del
Llanos, I can tell you that I am honored by their
friendship and feel distinguished by their trust. And
any one of them can teach honesty to whoever wants
to learn, because, my friend, the good name of a house
is locked up in its strongbox and isn't at the mercy of
the tongue of the first person who happens by."

"Bravo! Hurrah for Villegas! That ought to hold
him!" whispered Lara Rojas to his neighbor.

When the laughter died down Rodríguez spoke
again.

"Gentlemen, your oracle is the Yankee. You know
no other definition, and you have no reason to know
any other definition, of the word *business* than the
one the Yankees have taught you. Well, while we're
just killing time, I'd like to say that I, who, unlike
the rest of you, am not a human cash register or office
mouse, can give you a different definition of the word
business, not the one invented by the spoilers, but by
the despoiled. And don't laugh! One of these days
soon it may turn out more seriously than you think."

The group had stopped at a corner before dis-
persing.

"Just one more word, gentlemen."

Rodríguez' thin face had taken on a strange, proud

look. His near-sighted eyes glinted behind his thick glasses. His lips and the lines of his face trembled slightly.

"He'll wind up in an asylum!" thought Lara Rojas to himself.

"Just one more word, gentlemen. See if the definition of the despoiled isn't interesting. 'Business is our work turned into money for their pockets!' That's what millions of men are saying who are slowly beginning to realize where they stand. Good evening, gentlemen!"

CHAPTER V

Lara Rojas, seated at his roll-top desk, was addressing a pile of envelopes which he was about to fill with the announcements of the new firm of Del Llano Bros., Inc.

Nine days had passed since the death of Don Juan José del Llano. Nothing suggested him now but the black corners on the announcements and the black crepe bows on the lintels of the doors which the wind and dust had transformed into colorless rags.

A humble-looking woman in a shawl entered and glanced about. She asked to see Don Ignacio del Llano. Lara Rojas motioned her to a chair.

Her eyes took in everything: the doors of the house, now wide open, the newly waxed floors, the polished and sweet-smelling filing cases, tables, and chairs. She rolled her eyes and sighed meditatively.

A rancher in white duck trousers and gray hat and jacket came in and also asked for Don Ignacio. He sat down.

The little old woman was bursting with talk.

"What a heavy blow for the señores!"

She sighed again, but Lara Rojas gave no sign. The rancher, hat on knees, continued his examination of the print of the Eiffel Tower on the office wall.

Villegas arrived in great haste, his hat on one side, his vest open.

"Hello, hello, Don Boni! You beat me. I've been looking for you. Hello, everybody!"

The rancher stood up.

"Don Ignacio is on his way down," went on Villegas. "Of course you brought the papers, Don Boni?"

"Papers? We didn't say anything about papers."

"But, Don Boni, you know we can't do business without papers. There can't be any mortgage. . . ."

The rancher's face registered surprise and annoyance.

"What mortgage?"

"Of course, Don Boni! It can't be helped. But don't get your back up. Everything will be arranged. Don Ignacio's cash box is open for you, but business is business."

The correct figure of Don Ignacio, in heavy black, appeared. The little old woman and Lara Rojas stood up respectfully. Don Ignacio greeted them and led Villegas and the rancher into his office.

"What fools these ranchers are!" observed the little old woman. "They expect to do business on their word of honor. The Del Llanos are perfectly right to be so particular."

Once started, she could not be stopped. She asked Lara Rojas about his position in the Del Llano family, how much they paid him, what his monthly expenses were, and how his health was and that of his relatives. When she learned that he was the confidential clerk of his chiefs, the private secretary of Don Ignacio himself, no less, she no longer held back her own history.

"I'm an ailing old woman and one of these days the Good Lord is going to remember me and take me away. So before death slips up on me I want to make my will and leave my few pennies to our Holy Mother Church. I spoke about it to Father Jeremiah del Llano and we agreed that the best thing to do would be to deed my property to some wealthy and God-fearing person of good character. And who better than Don Ignacio himself? In that way I can keep my money from falling into the hands of the government or my relatives, who are just waiting for me to peg my hide out to dry. Don't you think it's a good idea? Of course, I'm not the first one to do such a thing, as you know very well. Lots and lots of others have done so. There was the Reverend Mother Inés and Sister Catalina de Jesús, who were millionaires, and my good friend Doña Ruperta Torrecillas, and Don Nicomedes de la Peña, and any number of others. . . ."

Her recital was interrupted by Rodríguez of *La Continental.*

"Is Don Ignacio in? He is? Good! I'll wait."

Rodríguez unfolded a newspaper and went to the window to read it.

"What are you, Rodríguez," asked Lara Rojas, "a Maderista or a Porfirista?"

"Why, naturally, I'm a Maderista, at least for the moment."

"All the mob are Maderistas," observed Lara Rojas. "But, as you say, it's better to be a Maderista for the moment. Fixed and unshakable principles always!"

"Look here, Lara Rojas. At the moment Maderismo is the revolution, and every revolution is necessarily inspired in justice and carries with it the aspiration for justice that every honest man has in his heart. But suppose that Maderismo triumphs, that Maderismo commits suicide by turning into government—for government is nothing but the regulated injustice that every rascal has in his heart. Then is it illogical to be a Maderista today and an anti-Maderista tomorrow?"

"What nonsense! That's anarchy!"

"Don't lose your temper, Lara Rojas."

Don Ignacio's door opened and Villegas and the rancher came out arm in arm. Rodríguez started forward, but turned at the sound of a young voice. It was Esperanza Viñas looking for her father.

"He never gets here before twelve," said Lara Rojas shortly, without raising his eyes.

Esperanza reddened and turned to go, but Rodríguez approached and held out his hand.

"How pretty you look this morning, Esperanza!"

"And how gallant you're getting, Rodríguez!" answered the girl mockingly.

"Yes, I am gallant, certainly, especially if you compare me with some parties who've got no more manners than a chimpanzee!"

Esperanza shot a sidelong glance at Lara Rojas and thanked Rodríguez with her small and intensely expressive eyes.

"Good-bye! I've got to run along. The workmen have been waiting for Papa for two hours and I can't find him."

"Let them wait. Tell me who you got all dressed up for."

Esperanza glanced down at her gray skirt, which was closely fitted to her shapely body.

"What a question!" she answered, with a flash of her small white teeth. "For you, of course!"

"For me? Or Ricardo de Lara, possibly?"

Esperanza wrinkled up her nose. Rodríguez put on his glasses and fixed his sharp eyes on her.

"Bah! That fool of a Ricardo? With his waxy face and his corn silk hair?"

She turned red and bit her lip.

"Excuse me, Lara Rojas! I forgot that Ricardo is a nephew of yours. It's all the fault of this devil of a Rodríguez. He loves to make a person talk too much. It was only a joke, Lara Rojas. Don't be angry."

Esperanza pulled her nose and shrugged her shoulders, while Rodríguez burst out laughing. But Lara Rojas seemed to notice nothing in his fury of working.

"Rodríguez," said Esperanza, suddenly serious, beckoning him away from Lara Rojas, "Rodríguez, what difference does it make to you whether I've got a boy friend or not, or whether it's this one or that one? You never miss a chance to ask me about it. As if it meant anything to you!"

"It's very easy to explain. It was only yesterday that you were a little girl and I carried you in my arms and gave you candy and taught you to talk and play with your dolls. So I don't see why I shouldn't teach you to play with your new . . . ah . . . toys."

"Well then, dear teacher, be pleased to understand that I haven't got a boy friend and don't want one, because the only man I'd have for a husband has got something the matter with him, something as big as a house."

"Come, Esperanza, tell me who he is."

"Wouldn't you like to know! Well, he's old, ugly, and what is worse, he's poor!"

"Good Lord, Esperanza, you frighten me! You're not getting personal, are you?"

Esperanza burst into a fresh and musical laugh and fled, leaving behind her a fragrance of soap and water.

"So, Rodríguez," said Lara Rojas maliciously, "still at your old tricks? Your little friend is pretty, for a fact."

"Esperanza is homely, friend Lara Rojas, but she's got something that others lack, a head and a heart."

"Homely, man! She's very distinguished-looking, an authentic type of the heroic Aztec race. Too bad she uses make-up. It couldn't be more unbecoming."

"You're a fool, Lara Rojas!"

The office door opened and Don Ignacio appeared, chatting amiably with the little old woman. Rodríguez gave him some papers to sign.

"Has Don Juan Viñas been here, Lara Rojas?" asked Don Ignacio. "If he comes tell him I'll see him at the job."

Rodríguez stayed only long enough to arrange his papers. Lara Rojas went on tirelessly addressing envelopes.

"Don Ignacio went on ahead," said Rodríguez to Don Juan Viñas, whom he met half a block from Don Ignacio's office. "That's his carriage. He's gone to wait for you at that great work you're building."

Don Juan lifted his hands in despair.

"But why didn't he tell me? I should have come for him before his office opened. I'm so sorry! How mortifying!"

"Don't take it so hard, Don Juan. You've lost only a few seconds. We'll take this streetcar that's coming. I've got some business over your way and I'll leave you at the job."

"Oh my goodness! To think that Don Ignacio will get there first and won't find me!"

Don Juan resigned himself and boarded the streetcar.

"How's your project going?" asked Rodríguez.

Don Juan was silent. The car was moving with snail-like leisureliness and stopped interminably at every corner. His anxiety and impatience puckered his good-natured face which, with its frame of black beard, resembled the Divine Countenance.

"Tell me truly, Don Juan. Are you going to make anything out of this business?"

"Only two persons in the world, Rodríguez, have any doubt about its success, two persons, ha, ha, ha! who've got a pretty nerve to call their souls their own: you and my wife. There's some excuse for her. After all's said and done, what do women know about business? But you, Rodríguez, you who have grown old in business, how can you come at me with that kind of stuff? Don't you remember how, ten years ago, when I was planning to move from *El León de Oro* to *La Sultana,* you said to me: 'Don Juan, *La Sultana* is too big for you. You won't get enough out of it to pay the rent.' And my wife said exactly the same thing. Luckily I've never paid any attention to you or my wife in such matters, and that's why I've made a little money. Am I right, Rodríguez?"

"You're perfectly right," answered the clerk of *La Continental* humbly.

Rodríguez' gaze was vague and far away.

"I must be a rotten businessman," he went on, half to himself. "I, who hate clerking, have been at it for twenty-five years. And in those twenty-five years I've criticized every plan of my employers and laughed heartily at the stupidity of my chiefs and their kind. And lo and behold! While they go on getting richer and richer, the only thing I've got out of it is gray hairs! Certainly, this logic that I'm so proud of is only the height of illogic."

"My poor Rodríguez!" exclaimed Don Juan. "You've been wasting your time reading books and papers that lead you nowhere, that don't get you anything."

Rodríguez heard the voice of Don Juan as if it were far away and indistinct.

"It all boils down to the fact," he continued, "that my interior world does not correspond to the real world, or, what amounts to the same thing, I'm unadaptable, a failure. And yet. . . ."

The streetcar came to a stop and Don Juan rushed headlong after Don Ignacio's carriage, which he had just caught sight of near the building. In his excitement he neglected to take leave of Rodríguez.

Rodríguez watched him running through the cloud of dust and smiled to himself.

"And yet. . . ." he repeated.

CHAPTER VI

When Don Juan returned to *La Sultana* late that evening he was astonished to see rays of light streaming out through the crevices.

"Is that you, Juan? Just a minute."

"How you scared me, woman! What are you doing up at this time of night? Half past eleven!"

"You were so late that I thought I'd wrap up the money from today's sales."

Elena barred the door again and went back to her chore of rolling up coppers in pieces of paper.

The electric lights were out and the weak oil lamp on the counter filled the long room with shadows. Don Juan inspected all locks with great care.

"What!" he exclaimed. "Hasn't Esperanza gone to bed either?"

He stopped a moment to contemplate his daughter, who was curled up in an armchair at one end of the room sleeping peacefully, her arms on the counter and her forehead resting on her hands. He tiptoed back to his wife.

"What a turkey we've got, Juan!" said Elena, clicking her tongue. "And a soup fit for a king!"

"What about the pulque for Juanito's birthday

party?" said Don Juan, clapping a hand to his head.

"I knew you'd forget it, you've got so much to think about, so I ordered some from *La Xóchitl,* the freshest they had."

"Good, Elena! Good! The boy doesn't like any other kind. Now he can't complain that only his papa gets pulque and turkey on his birthday. I'd like to have had some music, but we're in mourning—the Del Llanos, you know. The little devil! He made me open my eyes with all that talk of his about the viceroys. As if I knew anything about viceroys! In my day they didn't teach us that kind of thing, only the ABC's, Father Ripalda's catechism, and Fleury's *Ecclesiastical History.* And old Chonito certainly did teach us the multiplication tables! He didn't know his right hand from his left, but nobody could touch him when it came to the tables."

"How I wish we could send Juanito away to school next year!" sighed Elena.

"You know perfectly well that it's out of the question just now."

"Last year it was so easy, so easy that we took it for granted."

"Last year I hadn't even thought of the job I'm doing now, you know."

Elena sighed again, but did not reply.

"It's just a matter of waiting a couple of years," added Don Juan, distressed by his wife's pain. "Inside of two years the rents will start coming in. You'll see, Elena! Our income will double and all we'll have to do will be to sign receipts and more receipts. The work has begun. Within a year, that is, by November or December of next year, it will be finished. Four months after that the apartments will be dry and ready to live in. And then, rents and rents!"

"And interest and interest," said Elena, by way of echo.

Don Juan gave a start.

"Do you refuse to understand me, Elena? Or don't I make myself clear?"

Don Juan passed his thick, calloused fingers through his tumbled hair. He scowled with thought.

"See here, Elena. For example. . . ."

He spread a piece of wrapping paper on the counter and began to trace lines and put down figures.

"The line AB represents the east side of the property, BC the north. Now observe: these lines are the boundaries. Each little house has its living room, bedroom, patio, and even a toilet and bath. Now then, twenty houses on each side makes eighty for the whole block. How much will each one bring in, Elena?"

Elena was busy arranging piles of coin in the safe, so Don Juan had to answer his own question.

"Ten pesos, of course. There's no question about it whatever. A house of that kind is a bargain at ten pesos a month. Well, what workman earning a peso a day wouldn't be willing to pay ten pesos a month for a good house? So eighty houses at ten pesos a month —how much will that bring in?"

"Eight hundred!" cried Esperanza, now wide awake and standing at his side. "Won't that be grand! Then I can buy myself a pair of high-heeled shoes, really high, and some sheer stockings like the ones Teresa del Llano wears. Poor thing! She's so ugly! Did you notice them at mass, Mama? Awfully good-looking, dull rose and as fine as spider web. Oh, and then I want a suit made to measure, not like this thing. I look like a servant girl!"

Pouting, Esperanza lifted her skirt and displayed a pair of broken shoes, buttons missing and soles bent.

Don Juan drew her to him and kissed her on the brow.

"Tomorrow you're going to *La Carolina* and buy yourself a new skirt and the best pair of shoes in the place!"

"Oh, Juan, Juan!" exclaimed Elena, aghast at such extravagance.

"Let me see your plans, Papa!" cried Esperanza quickly, to head off further discussion.

Pleased, Don Juan unfolded his papers again and repeated his exposition with more enthusiasm. Again he traced lines and made calculations: addition, subtraction, multiplication, and so many brick and so many tons of lime, and so much for labor. . . .

He laid the papers in Elena's lap. She had finished counting the money and was listening absently, her thin, lined face resting on a long hand coarsened by hard work.

"Forty thousand pesos!" went on Don Juan excitedly. "Forty thousand pesos, a few cents more or less, is the total cost of the village. Well, I've had twenty thousand deposited in the bank for the past five years, and I've got twenty thousand more in securities. So what's all the fuss about?"

"All I say," answered Elena, "all I say is that even though we aren't rich, we don't lack anything either."

"Mama," said Esperanza impatiently, "would it hurt anything to have two or three extra pesos a day to enter in your cash book?"

"That's all very well, as I said, but your father is going into a business he doesn't know a thing about."

"When Papa opened his store with a capital of fourteen pesos he didn't even know enough to sell caramels. You told me so yourself."

Enchanted with the girl's reply, Don Juan kissed her again. Elena bowed her head, without bitterness.

"May Our Lord keep the soul of Don Juan José del Llano in His holy peace!" exclaimed Don Juan piously. "I owe everything to him. I've never told you, Elena, how it happened. Well, one day I went to the bank to make a deposit and Don Juan José, who was talking with the manager, came up to me and said: 'Wait for me, Don Juan, and we'll go out together.' I was surprised. I'd known Don Juan José for a long time, but he'd never spoken to me before. A how-do-you-do once in a while and that was all. Well, we went out together and he said something like this: 'How does it happen, Don Juan Viñas, that you, a successful businessman, are content to leave your money in the bank at a beggarly four per cent a year? That's not being a businessman! Come along to my house and my son Ignacio will let you in on something better.' Heaven bless him!"

"Amen!" yawned the two women, and all three went silently to bed.

CHAPTER VII

Rodríguez' arrival was the signal for a riot. He was almost knocked down by a swarm of youngsters tumbling about in the patio. The wild shouts of Juanito and his companions brought out Don Juan, with a scoop of sugar in his hand.

"What's going on here?"

Elena and Esperanza, wrapping their shawls about them against the cold, came running from the kitchen.

"Oh!" cried Esperanza, her eyes shining. "It's only Rodríguez and Juanito's mob."

"Boys! Boys!" shouted Don Juan, laughing. "For goodness' sake stop it! Leave the poor man alone."

"Viva Rodríguez!"

"Viva Rodríguez!"

Rodríguez could hardly be seen among the mass of heads, arms, legs, and bodies that were clambering over him, even on his shoulders, as he was pitilessly robbed.

He finally managed to escape, hot and half suffocated, but happy, as the swarm of urchins on their bellies scrambled after their pine nuts, peanuts, walnuts, and hazel nuts, the spoils of victory.

At two they were all seated at the table.

"Why doesn't Elena come and eat with us?" asked Rodríguez.

"She's nursing Perico," answered Esperanza. "When

he gets hungry he flies into such a tantrum that no one can stand him."

Elena had retired to her bedroom. Her ample hips overflowing a wide cane chair, she opened her blouse to a youngster of three months who threw himself on the white round breast and drained it flat. Elena could hear the incessant chatter of the children, the deep laugh of Don Juan, the penetrating yells of Juanito, the sober voice of Rodríguez.

They had a picnic in the country to end the birthday party. A cart was packed with Juanito's friends and the clerks from *La Sultana*. Those of more consequence followed, some on horseback, some on donkeys.

"Be quiet now," recommended Don Juan. "What would the Del Llanos say if they found out that Juan Viñas and his family were going on a picnic while they are stricken with grief?"

"Don't let that worry you, Don Juan," observed the proprietor of *La Vencedora*. "In all probability the Del Llanos don't even remember your name."

"Nor your mother's," added Don Matías the money-lender.

In Don Juan's opinion the one was as envious as the other was evil-spoken, so he rode on without answering.

Juanito sat astraddle of the wagon tongue, beating the mules till he made them gallop. Esperanza joked with the clerks of *La Sultana*. Everyone was in a high good humor.

"What's the matter with you, Rodríguez?" said Esperanza. "We're all having a good time and here you are with a face as long as a saint's."

"For an Esperanza," answered Rodríguez in her ear, "a Ricardo."

Esperanza blushed, without precisely knowing why. Was Rodríguez actually jealous of the insignificant Ricardo de Lara?

Rodríguez, however, was gazing indifferently at the luminous sky as he dangled his legs from the end of the cart. He inhaled the pure country air in deep breaths, the coolness of the woods along the road, the perfume of ivy and mimosa.

The cart halted at the edge of a little copse and the boys and girls got off with the crock of tamales. The dignified members of the party stretched out in the shade of a half circle of ash trees, while the youngsters scattered to look for wild flowers for making wreaths.

"Look out, Don Juan!" cried Don Matías, passing his hand over Don Juan's eyes. "I just saw Don Ignacio del Llano jump in the bushes over there! Why think so much?"

"Yes," said Don Tanilo, "we've come here to unbend a little. Smooth out that frown and have some beer."

"Don Juan's got that model village on the brain and you won't be able to cure him until it's finished. Your health, everybody! The beer is top-notch!"

Don Juan, smiling now and a bit puffed up, began to talk seriously, the rest formed a circle.

He expounded his philosophy hesitatingly. What was his motto in his work? "Help yourself and I'll help you." What was his secret for making money? "Very simple. Patience and stick to it. You save a penny because with that penny you complete the stack of twenty-five. You save the quarter, because with four quarters you have a peso, and with that peso you complete your first hundred-peso note. And you watch that note as if it were the apple of your eye until it grows to be a thousand. And so on. Patience, honesty, and stick to it. That's the secret of the rich."

"So, Don Juan," said Don Matías the money-lender, "you really think that millionaires make their money working?"

"What a question! Of course they do! And if they didn't, then it was their fathers or their grandfathers," replied Don Juan, firm as a rock.

"Don Juan is right," said Rodríguez, who up to this point had remained silent, listening curiously to the turn the conversation had taken. "Don Juan is right, and Don Matías, with his insidious question, is right, too. It's just a matter of terminology. Don Juan calls selling rice and garbanzos honest work. Don Matías calls taking the product of the worker's sweat, the goods of defenseless minors, the money of incautious widows and helpless old folk, robbery—that is, taking the shirts off their backs with the help of the civil and ecclesiastical authorities. Some save their last year's garbanzos and mix them with the new crop, or they give short weight, or they fill their sausages with ground bone. And so on. The first ones don't waste their time on such trifles, but at a single stroke rob the simple souls that God puts within reach of their claws. The others consume their victims bit by bit. What I'm driving at is that their work, that of the first group as well as the second, differs in quantity, not in quality. Don't you think so, Don Matías?"

Don Juan was intrigued for a moment, dubious and not fully comprehending; but when he saw Don Matías laughing uproariously he sensed the meaning of Rodríguez' words and sprang to his feet frantically.

"Rodríguez, you lie, you lie!" he shouted. "If I didn't know what a joker you are I'd never forgive you. You lie! You lie! You like to pull my leg and that's all there is to it. Gentlemen, I swear to you by all I hold most sacred that I've never stolen a cent from anyone!"

Such candor and good faith shone through his words that no one dared answer him. Don Juan thought he had won by the force of his argument and let himself go completely. But his thoughts were confused and incoherent. His eyes betrayed the perfect innocence of his heart, and his fresh face, without a wrinkle in which to hide a secret, vouched for his incorruptible goodness.

"If faith works miracles," said Rodríguez, deeply moved, "will works greater ones. You are rich, Don Juan, and you will be richer. You deserve to be. Gentlemen, let's stretch our legs."

On the way back to town everyone was in capital spirits. Rodríguez and Esperanza, the better to view the landscape, walked together behind the cart. The sun was setting. Rodríguez absentmindedly began to talk to Esperanza familiarly, as he had done when she was a child.

"How beautiful the evening is! See how the telegraph wires are like festoons of light, and how the adobe huts have dressed themselves in purple. It's sad, this shadow that's falling over the fields, the sky with its purple plumes, the chill of the evening. . . ."

Esperanza smothered a sigh. After a few moments Rodríguez spoke again.

"Autumn evenings. . . . I am an autumn evening."
Esperanza felt the contagion of Rodríguez' melancholy, but, not knowing what to say, sighed again.

CHAPTER VIII

"We must distribute the alms among the poor, Ignacio," said Teresa del Llano, breaking the sepulchral silence that had reigned for several long minutes. "That was his last wish."

Teresa held her hankerchief to her eyes to keep the tears from spoiling her make-up.

Father Jeremiah turned his dead face toward her. Don Bernabé sucked at his cigar without raising his eyes. Don Ignacio, erect and impassive, kept his sphinx-like gaze fixed on the alabaster lamp that lighted the recesses of the dining room.

The four grave silhouettes harmonized with a huge mirror at the far end of the room and the baroque sideboard at the near end. The furnishings, ostentatiously austere, exuded a self-conscious air of aristocracy.

A servant placed a soup tureen on the table. Don Ignacio spoke.

"In what form is the donation to be distributed?"

"In money," answered Teresa promptly. "I've thought it all out. Anyone who needs help will bring a note from the parish priest, or a recommendation from some charitable person, and we'll do what our consciences dictate."

"The professional beggars, that is to say, those who least need help, will be the ones to benefit," observed Father Jeremiah in his thin voice, reaching for a steaming plate of soup.

"Well, in that case," replied Teresa, adjusting her napkin and pushing up the rings on her small plump fingers, "in that case we could endow some hospital for the poor, or some other charity. I thought of that too."

"Donations to houses of charity," said Don Bernabé at this juncture, "pass through so many hands before reaching their destination that their actual benefit is doubtful."

"Just as I said," added Father Jeremiah, a spark of interest showing in his usually bleak eyes. "In any case the professional beggars will be the beneficiaries, while the others, the truly needy who are ashamed to ask for help and who suffer all the horrors of poverty, will never get anything."

"Very true!" affirmed Teresa with some heat. "Widows of decent families fallen on evil days, unprotected orphans who find the doors of vice open for them. . . ."

Don Bernabé cast a sidelong glance at the enigmatic face of Don Ignacio and waited for his judgment.

"The proverb says," said Don Ignacio, "not to let your left hand know what your right hand doeth. So we are not so much interested in the person who is to receive the alms as in the manner of making the donation."

"Well," said Teresa, "I should select ten poor widows, but respectable, to receive the money in accordance with their needs."

"All right. Should they receive the money in a lump, or in small installments?"

"In a lump, of course. Who could stand the sight of a constant stream of gloomy faces at the door?"

Teresa straightened up haughtily and arranged her false curls with the ends of her yellow fingers.

"That's not the main reason," corrected Don Bernabé, with energy. "It has always been an inflexible principle in our family never, on any pretext, to incur an obligation, big or little, ours or anyone else's."

All assented respectfully. They had forgotten one of their own dogmas.

"Then we shall have to pay it all in a lump," said Don Ignacio. "Well, then, giving the money in a lump will be the same as throwing it into the creek. Let's suppose, Teresa, that you've got at your disposal a thousand pesos with which to begin the work. What would you do?"

"Without any hesitation whatever I should begin with María Amarillo, the widow of that old bookkeeper of ours who died of consumption last year. They're living in the most frightful poverty. She came here yesterday with her oldest daughter, a girl of fifteen, to offer their condolences. There are eight of them, all told, and four are sick in bed with malaria. They've done wonders with the old clothes I gave them last year. But María is very thin and as pale as wax. She's beginning to cough already."

"All right," replied Don Ignacio. "If María Amarillo, who today hasn't got a cent to her name, receives enough to eat on for a week, the first thing she'll do will be to run to the market and lay in a stock of fruit, candy, sweetmeats, and dolls for the youngsters. And tomorrow María Amarillo will be wringing her hands because her children are sick and there isn't any medicine or bread in the house. And if you give her enough for a month she'll give a party and invite her friends. If she gets a year's allowance she'll pretend that she has to go to Sonora, or some such place, where she may possibly have some forgotten relative she'd like to visit."

"I can just see her," said Teresa, moved to tears.

"And," concluded Don Ignacio, "the next morning María Amarillo, in the most cruel penury, will be coughing, as she is coughing today, and will go on wringing her hands, as she is wringing them at this moment, at the sight of her children dying of hunger."

A servant announced the clerk Villegas. Don Ignacio wiped his mouth and went out to the corridor, where he and Villegas talked in low tones.

"Villegas has probably come," said Don Bernabé, "to tell us what happened to Ignacio's proposal to form a charity commission."

"What for?" asked Teresa.

Father Jeremiah explained that the crop failures of the past two years had forced the price of necessities up to the point where a laborer earning thirty-seven cents a day could not buy his corn and frijoles.

"What of it?" exclaimed Teresa, surprised. "The poor who lack corn and beans can always get prickly pears and are perfectly happy."

"That's true," said Father Jeremiah. "This is only an excuse to make trouble. I don't know who is responsible for making the rabble so ambitious that they're no longer satisfied with the lot that God gave them."

"Who else could it be," thundered Don Bernabé, his eyes flashing and his gray waxed mustachios trembling, "who else could it be but that bandit Madero, who promises to make them all rich, and, naturally, with the money of the rich! The doctrines of banditry are spreading everywhere. 'God didn't make the earth for this one or that, so let's divide it up!' "

"Communism!" assented Father Jeremiah lugubriously.

"However that may be," went on Don Bernabé, "the fact is that the cost of living is high, and it's also a fact that banditry is developing to the most alarming degree. So, until the government sends us troops to put down any attempt at pillage, we've got to keep the people quiet by bringing down the price of corn as much as possible."

Don Ignacio returned with a new and happier light in his eyes. But only for a few moments. His face soon reassumed the mask which sealed up his thoughts hermetically. Good news? Bad news? The only certainty was that it was news of some kind. Not even the saucy Teresa permitted herself the slightest question. All bowed before the severe discipline of the family, whose motto was absolute discretion.

After a prolonged silence Don Ignacio spoke.

"It may be that an opportunity has arisen by which we may comply with Father's last wishes better than anything we've thought of—perhaps very soon—perhaps tomorrow—in the charity commission."

The clock struck ten. They all rose solemnly and

Father Jeremiah gave thanks to God for all favors received during the day. The Del Llanos retired.

CHAPTER IX

The resolution of the charity commission was brief, but "it deserved to be engraved in letters of gold in the glorious annals of our country," as Lara Rojas said in his address.

When Don Ignacio rose to speak one could have heard a pin drop. His words were dry and had a metallic ring.

"I place at the disposition of the city government five thousand hectoliters of corn, to be sold at half the current market price. I permit myself to name the following conditions: first, that the sale of corn at a price higher than three pesos be prohibited for a month; second, that any person violating this agreement be fined the sum of not less than one hundred, or more than five hundred, pesos."

"Oh, the beautiful swindle!" whispered Rodríguez in the ear of his neighbor, Juan Viñas. "The swindle of charity!"

The proposal was approved by acclamation, and the vaulted ceiling of the council chamber echoed to thunderous applause.

Lara Rojas took the floor.

"Gentlemen, in the name of the very honorable city council, which I have the honor to represent, I wish to thank the great benefactor . . . the illustrious benefactor . . . I mean, rather, *our* great benefactor. . . ."

Lara Rojas coughed, cleared his throat, and blew his nose, to give him time to recollect the rest of his speech.

"Oh, blessed shades of Don Pablo del Llano, Don Lucas del Llano, and Don Juan José del Llano, who rest beneath the vaults of this august enclosure. . . ."

At this point Lara Rojas extended his right arm toward several portraits hanging on the walls, portraits of cross-eyed, long-nosed men, with mutton chop whiskers and prodigiously long necks, dispersed among the heads of Miguel Hidalgo, Benito Juárez, and Porfirio Díaz.

"The proverbial philanthropy of the Del Llanos. . . . Never did the needy go to them in vain. . . . Gentlemen, in your name I thank Don Ignacio and his very noble family for their many kindnesses to us."

"It is only the strictest justice," said Don Ignacio, "to inform you that you have nothing to thank me for, or my brothers. In the will of my father there is a clause, a legacy to the poor, in the sum of fifteen thousand pesos, and I, as the legal administrator of the estate, am making the bequest in this form."

The assembly could not contain itself and the applause thundered again.

"How many months are we going to eat rotten corn, Don Juan?" asked Rodríguez sardonically.

But Don Juan had taken offense at Rodríguez and did not answer, but made the sign of the cross with his hand hidden in his pocket.

For four months corn sold at three pesos—rotten corn, wormy corn, almost worthless, and, at the end of the fourth month and at one jump, it went up to six again.

Don Ignacio made an accounting to his brothers and sister. They met in his office in the still hours of the night. Don Ignacio opened books and Teresa jotted down figures.

"Bought, from García Rocha, of Tepatitlán, five thousand hectoliters of corn at two-seventy-five. Freight, cartage, commissions, etc. Total?"

"Fourteen thousand nine hundred and ninety-five pesos," said Teresa.

"Sold, to the city council, the same corn, at three pesos a hectoliter. . . ."

"Fifteen thousand pesos. Difference, five pesos."

"Good. The profit we should have made in this deal comes to exactly fifteen thousand pesos, since it was sold at half the market price. So we have distributed fifteen thousand pesos among the poor, thus fulfilling Father's last wishes. You can see that we've obeyed his will to the letter and have performed a general and equitable service. And all without taking a cent out of the cash box! But that isn't all. Put this down, Teresa. Five thousand hectoliters, bought during the sale of corn by the city council, at three pesos a hectoliter. . . ."

"But where did you find corn at that price?" asked Teresa, astonished.

"It was forbidden by law to sell corn at a price higher than three pesos, so our agents, Villegas and Lara Rojas, undertook to buy for the house all the grain that came in during those four months. So, put down five thousand hectoliters of corn at three pesos: fifteen thousand pesos. We shall offer this corn at the current price of six pesos. As you are beginning to see, we stand to make a net profit of fifteen thousand pesos on the deal."

"But," said Teresa, who was extremely punctilious, "we still have five pesos left to give to the poor."

"Exactly," answered Don Ignacio, closing the books and dropping the curtain over the office door. "Let Jeremiah spend them on masses for the peace of Father's soul."

PART TWO

THE RIFT

Porfirio López, baker by trade and president of the Twentieth of November Club, coughed importantly and twisted the half dozen bristles adorning his thick lips—hence his nickname, "the Pig".

"The meeting will please come to order. My friend Don Timoteo has the floor."

Don Timoteo, trembling with excitement, mounted the steps of the platform to read a sensational item in the daily paper.

*The Crybaby of Icamole has run away like a coward in the Ypiranga! Our great liberator, Francisco Madero, is on his way from the North to the capital of the Republic! We must have men in the government who are acceptable to the people. We should organize a program to welcome our great Redeemer at the railway station.**

Don Timoteo descended, perspiring and satisfied.

---

* Porfirio Díaz earned the nickname of the "Crybaby of Icamole," because he was said to have burst into tears after his defeat at Icamole, Oaxaca, during the War of the Reform. He left Mexico, after his overthrow by Madero, on the Ypiranga, May 26, 1911.

The assembly proceeded at once to appoint committees. The Rat was given charge of the balloons; Pedrito, a chimpanzee type who was covered with soot from head to foot, the fireworks; the Pig, the lanterns and torches.

A collection was taken up.

Don Timoteo observed that they had omitted the most important post, the orator of the day.

"I move the nomination of Señor Lara Rojas, who makes speeches in the city council," said the man who played the trombone.

Crispín, the news vendor, jumped to his feet indignantly.

"Is this going to be a people's celebration," he demanded, "or a caciques'?"

Don Timoteo replied that the Revolution had been won and that they shouldn't be too hard on the vanquished. He added that they were all children of God and that the greatest precept of the Ten Commandments was "that one about loving one another."

Crispín's objection, nevertheless, was unanimously sustained.

At this point the meeting was thrown into confusion by the rumor that an aristocrat had sneaked in. The Pig, with a flip of his finger, extinguished the candle on the rough pine table.

"It's Señor Rodríguez. He's a Maderista. He's all right."

The word traveled the length of the hall and put an end to the panic.

"Well, I propose," said someone, "that we name Felícitos Gallardo orator of the day."

The motion was received with applause. Felícitos

Gallardo was a member of the club and had been town orator for the past forty years. No high civic or ecclesiastical functionary, no personage in the world of letters, arts, or science, had passed that way without having had to listen to the solemn and cavernous voice of Felícitos.

Which is just what Rodríguez remarked in a low voice to his neighbor.

"Isn't he the gentleman," he asked, "who chants hymns to the Sacred Heart of Jesus at the parish school festivals and who a month ago received the bishop with such a pious speech that he won the honor of sitting next to him?"

Crispín, who overheard Rodríguez, at once got to his feet and repeated the words aloud. There was a murmur of protest.

"What's that got to do with it? Aren't we all Catholics here? Is this envy or charity?"

With rare tact Don Timoteo proposed that they decide the question by secret ballot.

"Felícitos Gallardo is unanimously elected," announced the Pig a few minutes later, stroking his bristles.

It was then proposed by Crispín that if Señor Rodríguez wished to make a speech on the program he might do so after Felícitos had finished.

Rodríguez had nothing to say.

"Then we have another question to discuss," said the Pig. "What do you think, should the speech be in prose or verse?"

He thought, personally, that prose would be preferable. Of course, he agreed that verse is a very high form of expression, but he thought Felícitos' prose was as clear and beautiful as the Lord's Prayer.

Crispín remarked that Felícitos was not going to address the general public, but Señor Madero and his illustrious company.

The question was still being debated when Felícitos himself came in and was greeted with a burst of applause, during which Rodríguez escaped unnoticed.

"Of course," pronounced Felícitos dogmatically, "of course verse is the more appropriate, or rather, the *only* way to do it. You should bear in mind that this will be an epopee!"

"That's a fact!" exclaimed Crispín and Don Timoteo in one breath. "An epopee!"

Pedrito, the fireworks-maker, inquired timidly if Mrs. Epopee was Señor Madero's wife, at which there was a great laugh.

The next day was set for the election of the city council and the meeting was adjourned.

CHAPTER II

"What's that row about, Lara Rojas?" asked Don Ignacio del Llano from his office.

The clerk went to the door. A crowd was milling in the distance. The national flag floated above a moving mass of white shirts, capes, and sombreros. Shouts of "Viva!" and "Muera!" could be distinquished in the hubbub.

"I know what it is, Don Ignacio," said Lara Rojas, laughing. "It's an election parade, sir. The Madero gang is electing the new city council. Ha, ha, ha!"

"I understand," said Don Ignacio dryly, blocking the door of his office and sending Lara Rojas back to his desk.

The shouting increased in volume as it came nearer.

"Death to the caciques! Long live the people! Long live liberty!"

"Don't you think we ought to close up while they're passing?" asked Lara Rojas.

"You may leave if you're frightened," answered Don Ignacio.

The crowd filled the street.

"Long live Madero! Death to the caciques! Death to the robbers of the people!"

Don Timoteo was running back and forth shouting vainly.

"Moderation, gentlemen! All the *vivas* you like, but no *mueras!*"

A stone shattered a window of Del Llanos Bros., Inc. Lara Rojas, badly scared, hid his head in his desk.

Villegas entered hurriedly, redder than ever, and went straight to Don Ignacio's private office without stopping to speak to Lara Rojas. A little later, when the mob had passed, Don Bernabé del Llano came in sputtering.

"This is wicked! Frightful! Ignacio, we'll have to do something about this! The mob has won the election! Here are the returns! What impudence!"

With Father Jeremiah, who came with the parish

priest, all the brothers Del Llano were gathered together.

"It's unheard-of!" continued Don Bernabé. Where are we going to land if this keeps up?"

"In the pit!" answered Villegas, who up to that point had been too scared to speak. "This means the paralysis of business, the death of commerce, industry, and agriculture!"

"The country's going to the dogs!"

"Chaos!" exclaimed Father Jeremiah, shuddering. "The end of respect for society, family, and religion!"

"What is happening here is an abomination, your reverence," said Don Bernabé, twisting his stiffly waxed mustachios. "It is absurd that we, the healthy and honest part of society should be at the mercy of a lot of beggars! What do you think, Father?"

The priest looked about and smiled gently.

"I don't absolutely disapprove of this revolution, because it may bring back some of our lost rights; but the Church and God Our Lord would be more honored if this movement were not headed by that poor creature Madero, who is leprous with free thought, spiritualism, masonry, and heaven knows what all!"

The company stopped their ears in horror.

The door opened and Juan Viñas burst in.

"Gentlemen, the mob has won! The mob has won!"

"And whom did they elect?" asked the priest.

"President of the city council, Don Timoteo of *La Bandera Mexicana;* councilmen: Casimiro Bocadillo, Amado Borrego, Toribio de la Vaca. . . ."

"Stop! That's enough!" shouted Lara Rojas in great

glee. "The people have filled their bellies. Their hunger and thirst after justice is satisfied. Casimiro Bocadillo, tarts, cakes, and pork pies. Amado Borrego will shave you and trim and curl your hair. What's-his-name Vaca will play second trombone for you in the municipal band!"

"The victory of the vagabonds!" raged Villegas.

In the laugh that followed they all dispersed.

CHAPTER III

After leaving his work at *La Continental* Rodríguez was in the habit of stopping by at the Viñas' to see Esperanza. By that time Elena was tired of darning stockings, mending clothes, and ironing, and they would all go strolling together beyond the edge of town. While Elena rested under a tree, Juanito, like a young colt, frisked over the turf until he was winded, and then would join Rodríguez and Esperanza and listen to their talk as they wandered aimlessly about.

"Does Rodríguez really amuse you?" Elena asked Esperanza one day, wondering.

"A good deal of his talk means nothing to me. Some of it I understand pretty well. But the curious part of it is that I'm so interested that I don't notice the time going by."

Elena was uneasy. Lately, Rodríguez had been paying more attention to his appearance. He shaved every day. His collars were spotless. His clothes fit him very well and were always clean.

"What was Rodríguez talking so long about just now?"

"Oh, Mama, I can't explain it. He began by telling me to observe the changes in the evening sky, how one cloud looked like a clot of blood. Really! And how the horizon was like a topaz lake. Do you know what topazes are, Mama? The stone in Teresa del Llano's necklace is a topaz. And how the light was like a golden mist. And a lot of other things. And then he was so funny. He talked about space and how nobody knows anything about the universal soul. And then he said the revolution is going to fail, because the people aren't ready for . . . for . . . something or other. Anyway, Mama, what he meant was that the poor people won't be able to govern themselves without help."

Another afternoon they were walking out beyond the town. Elena held her handkerchief to her nose when they crossed an evil-smelling creek, but Rodríguez went into ecstasies over the solitude and silence of the ruined quarter. An old cat, mewing piteously, dragged itself out from among the loose stones of a wall. As soon as Rodríguez saw it he ran and caught the wretched animal in his arms and strode away without a word.

Elena was astonished, but Esperanza laughed.

"Didn't you know about his mania, Mama? His house is full of cats and dogs. Juanito says one of his dogs is so fat that its belly drags on the ground and its hair is black and soft as velvet. Rodríguez loves his animals more than he would his own children."

"He's crazy," observed Elena, and gave Rodríguez no more thought.

CHAPTER IV

"Aren't you feeling well, Juan?" asked Elena, seeing
that his lunch box had not been opened.

"Me? Not feeling well? Ha, ha, ha! Still, I certainly
was off this morning. When I got to the job I couldn't
do anything right. I started to watch the masons and
the dust strangled me and the noise of their hammers
made me dizzy. So I left them and climbed a ladder
up to where the plasterers were working, but I
couldn't inspect their work because the ladder seemed
to be giving way under me and my head was going
round so badly that I had to get down. My heart
was going bump, bump, bump. Like that. And then?
Oh yes. I saw a workman who was supposed to be
mixing mortar and who hadn't moved his hands for
an hour, and I couldn't say a word to him. I was certainly off! Fact is, I did a little figuring this morning
and found that the money is about gone. Caramba!
Double shifts for two months and the money pouring
out in a stream! Even a well will run dry if you take
enough water out of it, let alone a cash box. The job
is getting along, but not as fast as I'd like. Not half
a yard in a week! So I got excited and doubled the
men, and then, when I saw there wasn't enough money
to pay them this Saturday I broke into a cold sweat.
This confounded head of mine! Can't remember a
thing. Didn't even think of the Del Llanos! I was
counting on them to help me finish the job. But I
suddenly remembered them and presto! Everything's

fixed up! It was my off day all right. Look here!"

Don Juan extracted from his wallet ten banknotes of a thousand pesos each.

"Of course I don't owe anything! I'm good for a lot more than that. But, you know, they offered it to me and begged me to accept it. It would have been insulting to turn them down."

"And the security?" asked Elena timidly, after a brief silence.

"What security would Don Ignacio del Llano demand of me, Elena? You don't know how friendly. . . . Why, between Don Ignacio and me. . . ."

Don Juan, very red in the face, began to stammer and hesitate.

"That is to say, not security exactly. . . . You and I have to sign a bit of paper. As Don Ignacio says very justly, every man should keep his papers in order and death will never catch him unprepared. And that's all there is to it. Not that there's any need of papers between him and me."

"A mortgage!" said Elena, with a lump in her throat.

"Well, yes, a mortgage," admitted Don Juan.

Not knowing how to lie, he fell silent, but his heart, just as it had done that morning, again went bump, bump, bump.

CHAPTER V

"It's a fine plan and easy to carry out," said Father Jeremiah, "especially since we can count on the divine help of our Father St. Joseph and our beloved Lady of Guadalupe. Another glass, gentlemen? Our Hea‑venly Mother has promised her chosen people that she will never abandon them to the spirit of dark‑ness."

Father Jeremiah was unwontedly loquacious.

"Quite right, Father," replied the manager of the National Bank, embarrassed, "quite right, but we are strictly forbidden to do it. For the rest, you know that the Party can count on the moral support and the votes of the employees of the bank. . . . Your health!"

"The peons of my hacienda," added another speaker, "have got orders to obey all the instructions of our great National Catholic Party."

"I can say the same for the workers of my textile mills," said a third.

"My men are at your disposal," said a fourth.

"And mine!"

All the twenty-odd persons at the meeting pledged their loyalty to the new party in a toast.

Father Jeremiah spoke again.

"I profoundly regret, gentlemen, that you cannot accept my invitation in the form in which I gave it. And all because of your personal cowardice, your total lack of civic courage! Your health, Father!"

"You're making a nuisance of yourself, Jeremiah!" Don Bernabé whispered in his ear.

"Your health, gentlemen!" repeated Father Jere‑miah. "I say again that the bishop would have been very pleased to see the healthy part of the community personally, *personally*, you understand, gentlemen, form the executive committee for this district. But you offer your support as if you were lending us your daggers to commit murder! No, gentlemen! We are defending a just cause, a noble cause, and we don't have to wear masks!"

Don Ignacio coughed so loudly at this point that Father Jeremiah had to moderate his flow of eloquence. The parish priest, who had been listening quietly to Father Jeremiah's alcoholic outburst, came to the rescue of the Del Llanos.

"The gentlemen, Father Jeremiah, have reasons which we must respect. We should be satisfied with the offer of support which they have so spontaneously made."

"Why, you ecclesiastics yourselves," added the manager of the National Bank, "because of your holy calling are forbidden to take part openly in the work of the Party. And yet, are you going to be any the less fatly rewarded for all that?"

The priest smiled and drained his glass lovingly.

Meanwhile, without attracting attention, Don Bernabé had succeeded in placing Father Jeremiah between Don Ignacio and himself. Father Jeremiah reached for the bottle, but Don Bernabé yanked him back by the cassock.

"No more!" he said fiercely.

"I repeat, gentlemen," went on Father Jeremiah, stubborn as a mule, "I repeat that I am genuinely sorry. Another glass, gentlemen? We mustn't insult this Martell."

Don Ignacio and Don Bernabé turned livid.

Father Jeremiah got up and joined his friend from *La Carolina*. Sitting down at his side, he recited with great feeling: *"Stay me with flagons, comfort me with apples, for I am sick of love!"*

Whereupon the proprietor of *La Carolina* assured him that he knew some very nice girls, and wouldn't it be a good idea for them to go see them that evening?

The company continued drinking, and talked a great deal about anarchy, libertinism, and impiety, and about the caricatures of the ridiculous figure of the diminutive Francisco Madero of which the press was full.

"Oh, you'll have to excuse Señor Madero for not paying enough attention to affairs of state. He's too occupied with those playful spirits!" remarked the priest.*

"Ha, ha, ha! What a wit your reverence is!"

They all laughed till they slobbered.

"The triumph of the righteous is at hand!" pronounced Father Jeremiah, who had donned his Spanish cape. He took his leave, leaning on the arm of the proprietor of *La Carolina,* while, cheeks a-blaze, he repeated in a tremulous voice: *"Stay me with flagons. . . ."*

CHAPTER VI

Rodríguez was strolling some time later with Esperanza and Juanito on the grassy bank of the river. It had rained recently and drops of water fell on his head from the leaves of the weeping willows. He stopped abruptly and answered an inward question.

---

* Madero was a Spiritualist.

"Yes, Madero will fall. His government is crumbling, and with it the false prestige of our Mexico. . . ."

He opened his mad eyes with growing excitement.

"Yes, Madero's government is a failure. Countries governed by bandits need revolutions brought about by bandits. Sad, but undeniable. You only have to read the opposition press to see the intellectuals and politicians in all their nakedness—faithful copies of the cultured and wealthy classes. Disgusting! They stink of the mud because they sprang from it, they breathe it, they eat it, and in it they are reproduced. When they show themselves in the newspapers or in the courts, they make me think of toads escaping from their puddles, raising their ugly heads to the sun that blinds them. They are happiest in the light and they bask in applause. They don't even realize that then they look more monstrous than they do in their native mud with only their eyes showing!"

"And what about the caciques?" interrupted Juanito.

"The caciques? Man, if the others are toads, the caciques are simply the mud that the toads live in!"

"Death to the caciques!" shouted Juanito, decapitating with his slingshot every prickly pear they encountered.

CHAPTER VII

Don Timoteo, president of the Most Illustrious Council, made two resolutions. First, he would name Felícitos Gallardo secretary of the city government. Second, he would buy himself a derby hat. To implement the first resolution he had only to sign his name, but the second was a graver matter. There was Dolores, for example, who had remarked inelegantly that he needed a derby hat just about as much as he needed a second nose. But Don Timoteo's mind was made up. He relegated to a nail on the kitchen wall the venerable straw that had served him for two generations, and the second problem was solved.

"My family and my friends," he mused, "won't like my stylish new hat, but how much less will the caciques like the notion that I, Timoteo Oliva, am going to sit where the noble rear ends of their ancestors have rested! Well, someone once said something about the world moving on, and several other things I forget. I mean, these are days of progress, and revolution is revolution!"

Don Timoteo washed his face, shaved, set his new derby on one side of his shining dome, and marched off to the town hall, trying to imitate the dignified bearing of a Del Llano.

It so happened that on the same sidewalk Don Ignacio was approaching and, with Don Ignacio, a problem for Don Timoteo, president of the Most Illustrious Council. Should he yield to Don Ignacio? Yes, he would yield, but only to teach him a lesson and demonstrate that the common people had better manners than the caciques. On the other hand, could he, as president of the Most Illustrious Council, representative of the sovereign people, step aside for a cacique? Caramba! Still, when all was said and done, there in the street Don Timoteo was no more than Don Timoteo and, for that reason, *could* yield the side-walk. It would be different, for example, if they were in the council chamber. And yet, no, he would *not* yield. The cacique might take it as an act of servility, of fear, or inferiority. No! Timoteo Oliva, representative of the people, would *not* be the one to offer them such an affront. Certainly not. . . .

"Did Don Ignacio shove me off the sidewalk? I think he did. But then, did he do so absent-mindedly, or was it a premeditated act?"

Thus Don Timoteo communed with himself, somewhat taken aback by his sudden collision with Don Ignacio, who passed on by without showing any sign of recognition. Don Timoteo was answered by the cynical laughter of Lara Rojas, Villegas, and several clerks of *La Continental,* who had been watching from the office across the street.

Don Timoteo refrained from mentioning the incident at the town hall, out of regard for his personal dignity as well as for that of the people who had elected him. But early the following Sunday the Pig showed him a piece in *El Pueblo,* the local weekly.

We have been witnesses, he read, *of a brutal assault on the person of our Chief Executive committed by a stupid cacique. . . .*

A virulent paragraph followed, in which the caciques were excoriated and the people urged to enforce respect for their officers by every possible means.

"Well," said Don Timoteo, much mortified, "I shall have to go and thank the editor."

"That's just what I wouldn't do, my friend, if I

were you," replied the Pig. "The editor of *El Pueblo* is insulting the señores, and that doesn't suit us, because the señores will think we put him up to it. We're in bad with them already and this will put us in worse. The señores are the señores and shouldn't be annoyed."

"I see what you're driving at, but if anyone doesn't like it he can lump it!"

"I don't think it's a good idea to get the señores down on us. I think we ought to go talk to them."

"You can go talk to them, my friend, because *I* am going to thank the editor of *El Pueblo*!"

Don Timoteo picked up his derby, clapped it on his head with considerable satisfaction, and went out.

"My friend the Pig," he thought, "doesn't know the meaning of the word democracy or the sacred cause of the people. My friend is not a liberal. . . . Still, on the other hand, he may be right. The señores are the señores and should be left out of this."

It turned out that the editor of *El Pueblo* was Rodríguez of *La Continental,* a discovery that vexed Don Timoteo not a little.

"This Rodríguez," he said to himself as he left the printing shop, "is a queer bird. When I thanked him and even offered to invite him to give the official speech on the Sixteenth of September, he didn't say: 'Sit down, Don Timoteo, and let's talk about it.' In spite of which I tried to explain my doctrines to him and he almost laughed in my face, as if to say: 'Don Timoteo, you're a fool!' No, no! That's not the man the people need. Proud, infatuated, arrogant. . . . Well, what do you expect? After all, he was raised among caciques."

CHAPTER VIII

The debate was getting very heated. Juanito claimed the chairmanship of the meeting and Cuate was arguing that he couldn't be speaker and chairman at the same time. But, since Juanito was in his own house and had passed around the peanuts, apples, and seed cakes, he was elected chairman by acclamation.

Juanito tinkled a bell.

"The chairman will take the floor."

He had one of the boys replace him at the table and solemnly mounted the empty barrel that served as a rostrum.

The cane chairs from the dining room were arranged in a semicircle. At the back of the room, on a kitchen table covered with an old piece of carpet, stood the altar of the Fatherland, decorated with red handkerchiefs and an antiquated shotgun belonging to Don Juan.

The audience clapped loudly and fell silent.

"Gentlemen," began Juanito, "we are met here to celebrate the centenary of Miguel Hidalgo y Costilla. He was born on the Rancho de San Vicente, which belonged to the hacienda of Corralejo in the district of Pénjamo. His parents were Don Cristóbal Hidalgo and Doña María Gallaga. Viva! And long live the great Morelos and the heroes of our country! And death to Cuate and death to the caciques!"

Juanito got down from the barrel amidst shouts of

"Viva!" and "Muera!" and the next speaker mounted the rostrum.

After the meeting, Don Juan Viñas, who was home for the holiday, called Juanito to one side.

"Who taught you all that nonsense? Who's your sixth-grade teacher?"

"Why, Papa, that's all in the *History of Mexico* by Pérez Verdía. Haven't you ever read the history of Mexico? The teacher says the same thing, only we never believe anything *she* says. Why, last year she was saying that Madero was a bandit and a highwayman, and now she calls him 'the immaculate patriot' and 'our great president'! And that's just what she used to say about Don Porfirio Díaz. We used to believe her."

"But how about this 'death to the caciques' business?"

"Oh, that's not in the book, and I didn't learn it in school either. But it's true just the same. And don't think that it's only the common people who are saying it. You ought to let Rodríguez tell you about the caciques! Esperanza, come here and tell Papa what Rodríguez thinks of the caciques. Oh, they're bad, all right! All the money they've got is just the poor man's labor they've stolen. Isn't that so, Esperanza? And Hidalgo was an enemy of the caciques, and Juárez was too, and Madero. . . . But ask Rodríguez; he knows the whole story."

Don Juan was worried. The next day he came home with his mind made up.

"Elena," he said, emphasizing his words, "I don't want Rodríguez to set foot in this house again."

Elena was flabbergasted.

"I suspected what kind of dirty skunk he is," went on Don Juan, "but I didn't know he writes for the papers and makes speeches. Yesterday he spoke in the theater and insulted the señores. Imagine it, Elena! The señores! They're going to fire him from *La Continental*. I heard all about it at the Del Llanos' office. So you see I know what I'm talking about. I don't want him to come here again, understand? And if you haven't got the nerve to tell him, just say so and tomorrow I'll put a bug in his ear, even though we've been friends."

"Yes," answered Elena, "I think you'd better do it yourself."

Esperanza, who was listening in the next room, sent a note to Rodríguez the next morning.

I beg you not to come and see me any more, for reasons I can't put in a letter. I'll see you.

CHAPTER IX

After the meeting at the theater where Rodríguez had fulminated against the caciques, the members of the Most Illustrious Council were much agitated.

"We're in a fix, all right!" said the Pig. "It's too bad that my friend Don Timoteo ever invited this Rodríguez to talk. Did you hear him, Felícitos? He said that property is robbery and religion is a myth!"

"Socialism!" exclaimed Felícitos Gallardo, who had

been hurt by the applause Rodríguez had excited.

"He's spoiling the show," observed Casimiro Boca-dillo.

"He's getting us in bad with the señores," added the Pig lugubriously.

"They say he's an anarchist!"

"And that he doesn't believe in the chastity of the Virgin Mary!"

"Is that all! Why, he doesn't even believe in God!"

"Well, what I say," replied Crispín, "is that Señor Rodríguez said a mouthful!"

"No, Crispín! Just look at what's behind his words. It isn't just talk. Just think, if we get the señores down on us they'll send you to the penitentiary and they'll cancel their orders with my friend Don Timo-teo, and they won't buy my flour or lard!"

"Well, as far as I am concerned, they can go. . . . I'm not one of those who think with their bellies, as the paper says."

"I move," concluded Don Timoteo gravely, "that we insert a notice in the paper to the effect that the Most Illustrious Council for 1912 does not accept re-sponsibility for the doctrines of Señor Rodríguez. This isn't a question of hating anybody, or thinking with our stomachs, or anything like that. The plain fact is that his doctrines are not ours, and that's all there is to it."

With the single negative vote of Crispín, who re-signed that day from the Most Illustrious Council, the resolution was unanimously adopted.

CHAPTER X

Rodríguez read Esperanza's note and was troubled. Thoughtful and depressed, he entered *La Continental.* A whisper went round among the clerks, followed by an eloquent silence. Rodríguez spoke to no one, as was his habit when out of sorts. He picked up a letter he found lying on his desk and opened it. The clerks looked solemn. Rodríguez read it without a sign. Then he calmly lighted a cigar, took his hat and stick, and went to the cashier's window.

The cashier read the letter and nodded. He turned the pages of a ledger and put a package of bills into Rodríguez' hand.

"I'm sorry, friend," he said in a low voice.

Rodríguez counted the money and left as he had entered.

"Five hundred and eighty-seven pesos, the savings of fifteen years of work! That is to say, more or less enough to keep me from starving to death for several months while I'm out of a job. Fine! Now I've got to see Esperanza. But then what's the good of that?"

A boy passed selling papers. Rodríguez bought one and sat down on a park bench to read. At the first few lines he smiled sadly.

The Most Illustrious Council for 1912 does not share the irreverent views about Society, Religion, and Country that Señor Rodríguez expressed in his speech on the Sixteenth of September.

"Poor creatures!" Rodríguez said to himself. "Not only are they as low, intriguing, and malevolent as those on top; they're even more imbecile!"

Rodríguez gave himself up to one of his interminable sad soliloquies.

"Rodríguez! Rodríguez!"

"Oh, it's you, Esperanza! I was just thinking about you and looking for you."

"Sitting here? Did you get my note?"

"Yes. This is my unlucky day. First, your father kicks me out of his house. . . ."

"Who told you that?"

"Your face is telling me."

"No, that isn't true, Rodríguez. It's only. . . ."

"And then I get fired from *La Continental*. And then, finally, the big show. The Most Illustrious Council pronounced a curse on me!"

Deeply troubled, Esperanza tried to explain. Rodríguez stopped her calmly.

"Silly! There's nothing for you to worry about. This blow doesn't come from your father, nor does the other one come from *La Continental*. There's a master hand in all this and it's none other than that of the Del Llanos. Ah, the Del Llanos! I don't hold anything against poor Don Juan. But tell him from me, Esperanza, to look out for the Del Llanos! In my case they've taken everything I had: my job, my future . . . and you, which is what I regret most of all."

Esperanza blushed violently. Rodríguez, touched, took her hand and pressed it between his.

"What are we going to do now, Rodríguez?"

"We?"

"Yes, so we can see each other."

Rodríguez smiled at Esperanza's simplicity.

"It's no good. Just keep a warm spot in your heart for this old man who has loved you so much, always, ever since you were a little girl. There's no sense in our seeing each other. I had to see you and learn who turned me out of your house. Now I know and that is enough."

"And so . . . ?"

"And so, one of these days we shall meet again, some day like this, by chance."

"Very well, then. . . . Good-bye!"

Esperanza walked away, desolate.

"He doesn't love me," she thought, but she had not seen the tears in his eyes.

CHAPTER XI

Every afternoon, late, Rodríguez left his house. He could always be found wandering about through the most remote quarters of town, his head bare and lifted, as if to breathe the air from the country round about, his eyes vacant, noticing no one and nothing.

One day Crispín, the news vendor, met him.

"Señor Rodríguez, the game is up! Don Timoteo and his friends have gone over to the caciques. To-night they're going to elect a cacique to the state legislature. But if you'll come and talk we'll blow them higher than a kite! I can carry the district of Maravillas."

Rodríguez was still irresistibly attracted by politics. He promised to show up at the preliminary meeting of the Twentieth of November Club, which was to be held in the theater.

There was a quorum present. The candidate recommended to the club by the government was a personage with handlebar mustachios, very stiff and self-important, with pretensions of aristocracy. On the platform he assumed a stern look, spat through his teeth, and spoke haughtily.

"High politics is one thing you shouldn't bother your heads about. It isn't in your line. I'll make a comparison that you'll understand. Let's say you make cottage cheese one day so you can eat it the next. Well, you can't make politicians as you make cottage cheese, from one day to the next. If you named one of yourselves as candidate he'd be a laughing-stock. He'd be ridiculous. So content yourselves with electing your town council, which is all you've got to do with government. But legislators have to be professionals, experienced in politics, used to speaking and writing. I am an author and a journalist, and I've got letters of sponsorship from men high in the press and government. Let that be enough for you. For form's sake, then, give me your vote and you'll be doing your duty as honest citizens."

The speaker got down from the platform as pompously as he had gone up.

Don Timoteo looked about at the audience. Would any one be so bold as to attempt to answer the señor who had come all the way from Mexico City, who was a journalist, an author, and heaven knew what else?

The Pig pulled his long lip and bowed to the very floor with approval.

At that point Rodríguez, who was sitting among the spectators, rose to his feet.

"The honorable candidate of the government has given us a notable lecture on civic duty and has brought us the cheering news that we provincials are little better than idiots. We should regret it if the honorable candidate of the government left us without hearing that we are grateful to him and that we wish to send our regards to his . . . ah . . . family."

Rodríguez' words were received with tempestuous laughter, and the candidate, who at first had presented his back to the speaker, turned half around and glared.

Without changing his expression, Rodríguez continued.

"I mean, Mr. Candidate, journalist, writer, etc., etc., that we'd like you to tell your colleagues that we barbarians in the provinces have taken the liberty of forming our own opinion about them. We think that the most ignominious depravity that the Revolution of 1910 has exposed is an abject intellectual class that drag their bellies through the mire and lick the boots of everyone in high place. We know that there are two kinds of slaves in Mexico: the proletarians and the intellectuals; but, while the proletarians spill their blood in torrents to win their freedom, the intellectuals fill the press with their nauseating slobber. The ignorant poor command our admiration; the intellectuals make us hold our noses!"

Rodríguez spat with disgust, while a thunderous storm of applause burst from all sides.

Wild with rage, the candidate jumped up on the platform again. His huge mustachios seemed to be having an epileptic fit and his eyes were on fire.

"Gentlemen!"

A colossal whistling drowned him out.

"Gentlemen!"

He was answered by a crescendo of savage yells, cowboy whistles, hisses, and shouts.

When the candidate could finally make himself heard, the theater was empty.

CHAPTER XII

Don Juan got home from his model village late in the evening, his hair white with dust.

"Is the work getting along all right, Papa?" asked Esperanza at dinner time. "When are you going to take me to see it?"

"Oh, it's getting along all right. . . . Getting along."

Don Juan's voice, however, was tremulous and his glance uneasy. He looked at Elena like a whipped cur.

Elena gave no sign.

Don Juan had avoided being alone with his wife lately. He stayed at home only long enough to eat and sleep. Elena never questioned him or alluded to his project; but it was precisely her silence that Don Juan found unbearable.

"What are Juanito and Esperanza doing?" he asked

fretfully. "The band music is going to waste in the square and you youngsters are sitting around here as if you were seventy. Come! Quickly! Get off to the concert and leave us old folks at home by ourselves."

Don Juan spoke to Elena like a criminal who can no longer hide his guilt. Oh, the work was paralyzed now! He had done everything possible. The front walls were finished. Caramba, how pretty and graceful they were! But. . . . Oh, if Elena would only come and see them! Every little house with its door and two windows, and then another and another, twenty to a side. The loveliest little houses, all alike, pretty as Christmas toys! But. . . . Well, the money had got low again. Rather, it was gone altogether. That was to say. . . . But how pretty they would look when they were painted a light blue, their sides a slate grey with yellow trimming! It was a pity. . . . But, what the devil! They were almost finished. . . .

Don Juan spoke haltingly. Elena's stony silence drove him into a frenzy. He had to keep on talking to drown out that accursed stillness.

"What the devil! Really, the job doesn't need much more, only some lumber, doors, windows, a few roofs as well—most of them, in fact. But what of it! A wagon load of iron beams, two of boards and joists. . . . The principal cost, in fact, is the labor. With ten thousand pesos more, Elena, it's done!"

He stopped, faint and sweating.

"What do you say, wife? Speak, for God's sake!"

Don Juan fixed his agonized and pleading eyes on Elena.

"Don't borrow any more," she said gently. "With the store we've got enough to live on."

"What! And leave our fifty thousand pesos buried there!" shouted Don Juan, jumping to his feet, wild with desperation.

Elena answered not a word.

CHAPTER XIII

One night Don Juan came home so worn out that he left his plate almost untouched. The Del Llanos had refused to lend him any more money. He had managed to beg a handful of dirty bills out of them, a mere thousand pesos.

For hours he sat alone, thinking. He tried to understand what was happening to him. He sought some glimmer to illuminate his slow wits. Up to a certain point, he admitted, the Del Llanos were right. Things *were* very uncertain in business. Madero's government was going to pieces. Everybody knew it and everybody was scared. It was believed that a change would help the financial situation, but no one would risk a cent. That much was all perfectly clear. But why had the señores received him so coldly? Why had Father Jeremiah refused to speak to him? And why had Don Ignacio ignored him at first?

Don Juan made a minute examination of his conscience. He found himself guilty of no mortal sin. Bah! Not even a venial sin! Why, today, for example, he had eaten the same breakfast he used to eat twenty years ago, when he went about in a shirt and white pants: a bowl of atole and a plate of fried beans with chile. Milk? He didn't drink it even for medicine. His stomach didn't need it. So if his wealth had brought him any luxuries they were so trifling that it was hardly worth the trouble to remember them. He now had a seat in the orchestra instead of the second balcony, or, to put it another way, fifty cents a head more, four or five times a year. Once a year they gave a party. In strict turn it was given for himself, Elena, Esperanza, and Juanito. But the expense wasn't as great as you might think. Elena managed to borrow even the pan to cook the turkey in, and he, for three months in advance, watched his chance to pick up a bird at about half the market price.

He had no opinions. More accurately, his opinions were those of the señores, who knew. He went to mass on Sundays and obligatory feast days, like everyone else. Once a year, during Lent, he made his confession. When special services were got up for the señores, the first thing he did was to look for the name of the Del Llanos on the list, and if he found it he didn't hesitate to put down his own. When some committee asked him to lend his name to a petition or any paper of a political, social, or religious nature, he never bothered to read it. He merely looked at the signatures at the bottom, and if he didn't find those of the Del Llanos, he told the committee to bring it back when it had been signed by those who had always been his guides. He was the first to call on the newly elected city officers. He never missed banquets in honor of distinguished magistrates, governors, and bishops. Although he was always seated at a modest place at the table, he took no offense, because it was not vanity that brought him there, but a healthy desire to do everything that the respectable señores did.

His domestic life was spotless. True, he made his wife work like a slave, but he loved her with all his heart. He loved Esperanza, too, so much so that he had bought her a Rosencrantz piano, at fourth or fifth hand, and he gave Juanito ten cents every Sunday for the movies. But Esperanza paid for her piano with mending and ironing, and Juanito paid for his movies by collecting old accounts.

Don Juan, in fact, could accuse himself of no formal sin whatever, and his sad eyes gazed uncomprehendingly at the bundle of bills.

CHAPTER XIV

"Rodríguez used to come to see me only because he wanted a good echo for his voice. He needed someone who'd let him think aloud and listen to himself without interruption."

Thus mused Esperanza, after waiting three months for Rodríguez to seek her out. He hadn't even written to her. She had reached the point of making herself believe that she was getting used to the absence of her old friend and would gradually forget him. But, one evening, as she was coming home with Don Juan on the streetcar, her heart gave a leap when she recognized the man who got up to give her his place. Esperanza thanked Rodríguez and gave him her hand, but Rodríguez, proudly, without even glancing at Don Juan, escaped to the far end of the car.

Don Juan and Esperanza passed him as they got off and Esperanza slipped a piece of paper into his hand.

Tomorrow, at the same time, I'll be with Juanito.

Rodríguez was punctual.

"I'm very angry with you!" was Esperanza's greeting.

She installed Juanito in a front seat, while she went back and sat down next to Rodríguez.

"You're very ungrateful to those who love you."

"But. . . ."

"No buts! You're going to say that Papa and Mama and this and that and the other. Well, what of it? If I don't care, why should you?"

Rodríguez warned her that several of the passengers seemed to be listening, so Esperanza bravely proposed a rendezvous for the next day where they could talk freely.

They fell silent, but Esperanza soon burst out again.

"Didn't you lead me to believe that you were one of those rare spirits who can't pretend? Who never lie?"

"It's true. . . ."

"You pretended to love me, and what then? Nothing but lies! You think more of your horrible cats than you do of me!"

"Esperanza!" exclaimed Rodríguez, furious.

Esperanza was delighted, but her heart sank at his next words.

"Whoever speaks contemptuously of any of my little friends, is contemptuous of me!"

Rodríguez failed to notice the effect of his outburst

on Esperanza and continued talking. They made an engagement for the following day.

"Tomorrow in the Alameda at five sharp."

Rodríguez was so happy that he did not see the sadness in Esperanza's eyes.

The next day, very carefully dressed, Rodríguez was pacing up and down the Alameda impatiently. Esperanza had removed the barrier that he himself had erected between them and he no longer had any reason to disguise his feeling for her.

"My forty years mean nothing!" he exulted. "Nor my being a clerk out of a job! Nor my reputation as a red! Nor my dozen cats and my black dog! Esperanza, I love you! I worship you!"

Esperanza was at home mending clothes. She heard the clock strike five and counted the strokes one by one. "It's no good," she repeated to herself. That it's-no-good had been sticking in her heart ever since *that* day. "It's no good." Those were the words Rodríguez had said three months before, when, in the anguish of her heart, she had asked him to see her. "It's no good," was his answer and she, like a fool, had not understood the cruelty of it until this moment.

At six Esperanza was still thinking of Rodríguez.

"Yes, he does love me. He has never lied to me. But he doesn't love me as I love him."

Esperanza wept.

CHAPTER XV

Madero's government fell at last.

Lara Rojas and Villegas belonged to the respectable element. They had to get drunk and go out and celebrate. Which they did, along with a dozen bootblacks (hired at ten cents apiece), all wearing little paper tricolors and shouting at the top of their lungs: "Long live General Victoriano Huerta!" If they had felt any restraint in public, it was not so in the back room of *La Carolina,* where the glorious news of Madero's murder was celebrated with a great banquet. The air was charged with animation, cordiality, alcohol, and a great deal of talk.

"Let's congratulate ourselves for having found the iron hand that the country needed! Now we have a *real* government, a government of decent and honest people!" said Don Ignacio del Llano, putting into a nutshell the ideas that Lara Rojas and Villegas had been wrestling with for half an hour.

"It's too bad," exclaimed some simple soul, "it's too bad that such a good cause had to be spotted with innocent blood."

He was drowned out in a unanimous protest. Of course, some blood had been spilled, but if anything had raised enormously the prestige of the government it was that high act of national justice!

"But that is always ugly. It's a crime, to put it bluntly!" insisted the unlucky objector.

"It's an error to judge the execution of Madero as a crime," interrupted Father Jeremiah. "Regicide itself is approved of by the Church, as I can demonstrate. The very learned Fathers of the Company of Jesus have defended that thesis brilliantly. But I don't have to tell you about that. All of you, as well educated Catholics, are acquainted with that fine little book of Father Sarda y Salvany. You can injure, wound, kill, do anything you like, in short, if it redounds to your own good and *ad majorem Dei gloriam!"*

"What I can tell you, gentlemen," said another, somewhat unsteadily, "is that the news fell like a bombshell among the people. I saw the look on the faces of the mob at the time of the demonstration and, really, I shouldn't advise you to be so carefree and happy over the business."

This was a wet blanket. Enthusiasm diminished to the vanishing point. Faces clouded over.

Someone said that secret meetings were being held in Don Timoteo's store.

"My cook has seen masked men going into *La Bandera Mexicana* night after night, about nine o'clock."

The company discussed the possible meaning of it. It looked highly suspicious among men who had already shown they had political ambitions. Beyond any doubt whatever the purpose of the meetings was to gather arms and ammunition. Imagine such an arsenal in the hands of a lot of bandits, while respectable people were utterly defenseless! Why, the blow might fall at that very moment, while they were trusting to the protection of a real government! What could be easier than for the bandits to attack them that same night, tie them up, rob them, violate the virgins, the near-virgins, the ex-virgins, and then murder them all!

The company stood and raised their hands solemnly to heaven.

CHAPTER XVI

Lara Rojas burst into Don Ignacio's office, beaming, bearing a sheaf of newspapers.

"Here's the proof!"

The detective adjusted his glasses and held out his hand for the papers, but Lara Rojas was too excited to relinquish them.

February 20, 1913.—he read—*The caciques are holding a public celebration today over the fall of Madero's government, the very day that we hear of the murder of the President of the Republic! Now that his government has fallen, the vultures are fighting for a place among the circle of thieves and fools, croaking and leaving their droppings on his body!*

"Those are personal insults, don't you think?" said Villegas to the detective.

"Oh, you haven't heard the half of it!" went on Lara Rojas. "Just listen to this!"

February 27. A half-drunken blacksmith met me in the street and said: "Chief, they've killed our Señor Madero! What a shame for Mexico! What traitors we are!" He seemed to take some pleasure in repeating this last phrase in a hoarse and broken voice, with tears in his eyes. One thing I am sure of is that Mexico will wash away this stain! Yes, she will wash it away!

"Give me those papers. That last is enough," said the detective. "What did you say his name is? Rodríguez? Good!"

"But wouldn't it be a good thing to arrest the blacksmith at the same time? An accomplice?" observed Lara Rojas.

"Do you think that's enough?" asked Villegas.

The detective, however, refused to commit himself, but they all felt that their hopes would soon be realized.

CHAPTER XVII

Don Juan was startled by two sharp knocks at his office door.

"What a fright you gave me, Lara Rojas! It's funny, but that has happened to me three times today. Any noise at all makes my heart jump out of my mouth."

Lara Rojas sat down, after a disdainful glance at the white-washed walls and worm-eaten beams of the room, and the chromo of the Virgin of Guadalupe at one end, its only decoration.

"I came," he said, "to tell you about the banquet that we're giving tomorrow for the agent of the secret police from Mexico City."

Don Juan frowned.

"We're going to smash the gang," explained Lara Rojas.

Don Juan looked at him again, still puzzled.

"Well, but . . . what's that got to do with me? I don't meddle with politics."

"This isn't politics—simply self-defense."

"I don't know what you're driving at, Lara Rojas."

"It's plain as day! This is a banquet that respectable society is giving to an individual who's coming to defend them."

"Are the señores in on it, Lara Rojas?"

"Are they *in* on it! Why, they're the ones who are getting it up!"

"Why didn't you say so in the first place?" exclaimed Don Juan, patting Lara Rojas on the shoulder. "If the Del Llanos are running it there's no reason to ask my opinion."

He put his fingers into his waistcoat pocket.

"How much is my share?"

"Twenty pesos, Don Juan."

"Good! Very good! Here you are! And now, Lara Rojas, tell me what this policeman from Mexico City is up to."

Esperanza, who was sewing on her machine in the next room, stopped her work and listened.

CHAPTER XVIII

Escape! You're going to be arrested!

Rodríguez read the wrinkled bit of paper that a boy

handed him as he entered his house. It bore no signature, but the handwriting was very familiar. Rodríguez kissed it.

He felt at first that all his strength had left him. Then came a feverish reaction. The choice he had to make was between the useless sacrifice of his life and the Revolution.

It was ten o'clock and raining. The street was dark and deserted. At a corner the greenish eye of a lantern shone and blinked out immediately. Rodríguez hesitated. Should he return to his house or keep on? He stopped, eyes and ears alert. At the crossings the streaming rain shone in the light of the street lamps. He heard distant footsteps. He had an impulse to draw his revolver and hide in a doorway. He remained standing where he was.

A boy, wrapped in a blanket, crossed the street, hugging himself against the cold. A dripping dog slunk by at a trot.

Rodríguez decided to go on. He walked two blocks along a street leading to the outskirts of town and stopped again, fearful of what might be hidden in the black shadows of a garden. In front of him rose the gray mass of a church with a single tower. He saw a tiny red light in the distance, perhaps a hut lost in the darkness. It was nothing—silence, nothing more. Among the heavy black clouds an unexpected star shone out.

At last Rodríguez felt he could breathe and set out resolutely. As he rounded a corner a heavy hand fell on his neck. He was looking into the green eye of a policeman's lantern, along the shining barrel of a pistol.

CHAPTER XIX

"This is the place!" whispered Lara Rojas to the detective.

They advanced on tiptoe to the house and put their ears to a window.

"We've got them!" exclaimed Lara Rojas excitedly, rubbing his hands with satisfaction.

It was Don Timoteo's house, behind *La Bandera Mexicana.* Felícitos Gallardo, Crispín the news vendor, Casimiro Bocadillo, and five or six others entered, one by one.

"We've got them!" said Lara Rojas over and over again, sweating in his agitation. "Isn't it time to take them in?"

"I've got to listen to them," replied the detective impatiently.

He looked through the window. The room was small. The only light came from the thin rays of a street lamp penetrating the shutters of the half-open window. Don Timoteo sat hunched up in his cane chair in the shadows. Everyone inquired about his health. He said he was better; but his asthmatic breathing filled the room and he was strangled by frequent fits of coughing.

The group sat for a quarter of an hour in silence, with bent heads. Don Timoteo forced himself to speak.

"Our father has been killed!" he stammered in a choking voice.

They all wept.

Without, a cold February wind was blowing. A street band somewhere was playing "Las Mañanitas de Madero".

PART THREE

DIES IRAE

CHAPTER I

It was growing dark. The last workmen were leaving. In the quiet and solitude Don Juan contemplated for a moment the scaffolding woven of beams and boards, the brick walls, still fresh, the mixing trough, wet and white with the remains of the last batch of mortar. The empty doors and windows were half in the shadow and half in the light. The houses were still roofless.

Don Juan stood gazing at his work for a few brief minutes. His heart was heavy and he felt he was leaving a part of his very being there. With sudden clairvoyance he shook his fist at the city, dimly seen to his right. But the city, peaceful and silent, answered his curse with a murmur of far-off voices, the laughter of children, the braying of a donkey, a bugle call from the barracks, the faint crowing of a hoarse cock. . . .

The next morning Don Juan took his place behind the counter of *La Sultana*, alongside Esperanza and Juanito. He had thanked his clerks and told them the house could no longer afford to pay their wages.

During the first day the customers hardly noticed the presence of Don Juan, so great was the sensation

caused by the arrests made the night before. Don
Timoteo, Casimiro Bocadillo, Felícitos Gallardo, and
a dozen other members of the Twentieth of November Club had disappeared. Rumor had it that they
had been tied together, led out, and shot. One customer was sure he had heard the sound of firing
early that morning; another, that he had seen a patrol
of cavalry with the prisoners in their midst.

In the afternoon a charcoal burner coming in from
the mountains reported he had seen the prisoners
marching on foot, tied by the wrists.

"Was Rodríguez among them, who used to work at
La Continental?" asked Esperanza carelessly.

"I don't know the gentleman, miss."

Don Juan glanced at her inquiringly.

Later that evening one of the plasterers from the
model village came in to buy a candle.

"What, chief? You back in the store? When are we
going to finish the job? It's a good job, no matter
what they say. Pity it costs so much money. . . . Did
you hear that last night they blasted a poor devil out
behind the cemetery? I live near there. I heard a commotion about daybreak and got up to see what was
going on. It was too dark to recognize anyone. Anyway, they took a fellow out and, bang! They shot him.
Poor devil! They even had his grave all dug. They
left soon afterward. When it got light I went over to
see. God have mercy on his soul! The earth on his
grave was still loose. I made a cross out of a couple
of sticks and said a pater noster for him."

From the beginning Esperanza had guessed the
truth. She turned white and her legs trembled so vio-

lently that she had to lean on the counter to keep from falling.

CHAPTER II

When the excitement began to stale, the customers of *La Sultana* took to greeting Don Juan with the same question: "How's your model village getting on, Don Juan?" They did so without any thought of malice, but for Don Juan it was a pitiless ordeal the whole week long. Lacking the courage to face it, he retired to his room at the back of the store. After all, Esper- anza and Juanito were quite capable of looking after the trade. But the torturing questions penetrated even into the back room. "And how's Don Juan, chil- dren? Is he working again at his model village?" Don Juan fled to the remotest corner of the house. No one dared to speak to him about the merest trifle. His grief imposed respect. Weeks passed; a month, three months. The first payment on his note came due.

Don Juan shook off his stupor, asked for clean clothes, shaved, and combed his hair.

Elena remarked that he was very pale. Esperanza said that although he was eating so little, his cheeks and eyelids looked fat. But it was an unhealthy fat: his color was ashen, his cheeks hung limp and flabby, his eyelids were merely puffy.

"It's because he's been shut in so long," was Juani- to's opinion. "You need some fresh air, Papa."

"You're not eating enough, Papa," added Esperanza. "We ought to call the doctor and get him to prescribe some iron for you. A friend of mine was helped a lot by it."

Only Elena was silent, as always.

Don Juan called first on Lara Rojas, who had just gone into business for himself.

"I've got a nice little proposition for you, Lara Rojas," said Don Juan, putting up a brave front and making an effort to appear his old frank and jovial self.

Lara Rojas hardly lifted his eyes from his papers.

"Oh, it's you, Don Juan. I know what your proposition is. You'll have to excuse me. Too much to do. And anyway, it belongs to the Del Llanos. You know I owe them everything I've got."

Don Juan agreed. Lara Rojas was more than right. Gratitude was more important than anything else. A man who isn't grateful can't be honest. Caramba! Lara Rojas might be ill-mannered, but he was grateful.

"Lara Rojas, give me your hand! That's the kind of man for me!"

He pressed Lara Rojas' hand warmly.

Next he went to see Villegas, but Villegas found himself under the same obligations as Lara Rojas. Villegas also was right in refusing, so Don Juan approached the proprietors of *La Carolina*.

"We stand in very well with the Del Llanos," the head of that firm explained, "and it wouldn't do for us to offend them. Your business belongs to them by right. If we can serve you in any other way. . . ."

The worst of it was that everyone Don Juan spoke

to gave him the same answer: they all had excellent relations with the Del Llanos and could not run the risk of their disfavor.

"See here, Elena," said Don Juan to his wife when he got home, "explain to me why everyone I speak to about taking over my project comes out with its belonging by right to the Del Llanos."

Elena would have liked to speak clearly, to tell him that those fine friends of his, so fraternal, so grateful, so honorable, were just like any other gang of highwaymen; but, resigned as always, she attempted to console him.

"It's because you owe the Del Llanos money. Sell them the property. It won't make any difference."

"I was sore at the señores because of the way they treated me the last time I saw them. But if you think best. . . ."

CHAPTER III

Don Juan came home in a cab, beaten, and went straight to bed, his eyes dull and his stubborn head bent, like that of a bull wounded to death.

Juanito wanted to send for the doctor, but Don Juan shook his head slowly. What good could the doctors do him? He asked to be left alone with Elena.

"Ruined!" he stammered.

The Del Llanos? They had disowned him. When he mentioned his business Don Ignacio had laughed. "What a country we're living in, Don Juan! Our branches in Monterrey, Chihuahua, and elsewhere are closed. The bandits are threatening Torreón. Exchange was at thirty this morning."

Deuce take it! Of course they were fond of Don Juan! But business was so bad they couldn't take any risks.

"The only thing we can do for you is to accept your stock against your debts—everything, of course. The firm will be doing you a favor that any merchant would appreciate. You understand? We can save you from the worst, from the disgrace of bankruptcy."

A chill had penetrated to Don Juan's very bones, such a strange chill that his hands and feet seemed to be paralyzed. His tongue refused to obey him. Don Ignacio left him standing there and went to serve a customer. Don Juan dragged himself with great difficulty to the office door, hailed a cab, and came home.

CHAPTER IV

A month later the employees of the firm of Del Llano Bros., Inc., in brand new uniforms, took possession of *La Sultana*. In the morning they removed the stock, in the afternoon all the furnishings of the house. Esperanza, even when she saw her piano going, was unable to take in the magnitude of their ruin.

Finally, when there was nothing left but a few torn and unserviceable mattresses, Don Juan and his fam-

ily were left in peace. And then it was that Elena
drew herself up, straighter, stronger, more serene.

"Don't worry, Juan. We've got as much now as we
had twenty years ago. No, I'm wrong. We've got more.
Look!"

Elena drew the heads of Esperanza and Juanito to
her breast and kissed them through her tears.

"We were happy then. Why shouldn't we be happy
now? To work, to work, everybody!"

Don Juan pulled up his trousers a little to show his
swollen legs and pressed Elena's hand to his heart,
which was beating like a tired bell clapper. A single
tear shone on his lashes.

"Too late!" he said very quietly.

CHAPTER V

"Sweet name of God!" cried Crispín, as he caught
sight of Don Juan under a street lamp. "You, Don
Juan, in this state?"

Don Juan was leaning on Esperanza's arm. At every
step he stopped for breath, and at every breath he
lifted his thick black beard and swollen eyes.

He explained. They were moving to their new
house. They could no longer pay the rent for the old
one. They were going to live on Alacrán Street, some
fifteen blocks away. It was cheap. Esperanza was earning eight pesos a month and Juanito four. Himself?
Well, you could see the fix he was in!

"Bandits!" shouted Crispín furiously. "This is the kind of job they know how to do so well! But why are you moving so late at night?"

"We're not made of stone! After all, we've got a little pride left."

Two great tears rolled down Don Juan's cheeks.

"Don't talk that way, Papa," said Esperanza. "Look, sir, my father's determined to see everything on the dark side. True enough, we're poor and the only things we've got left are in these two bags. But, as I've already told Papa, he started out even poorer than that. The fact is that if we hadn't run into some hard luck in this last business. . . . Juanito and I have hardly begun to work. Don't you think Papa is wrong to take it so hard? That's what made him sick."

"Hard luck? A curse on the bandit caciques! I know well enough what has happened to Don Juan!"

Crispín cursed and spat.

Don Juan raised his mild eyes and fixed them for a moment on Crispín, reproachfully.

"Oh, don't talk to me about *them*, Don Juan!" answered Crispín. "Those bandits have ruined you! Bandits, bandits, bandits! I'll say it even though they tie me up again and take me to jail!"

"You mustn't say such things, Crispín. It's the will of God. Who are we to oppose the working of His Divine Providence? Blessed be His Holy Name!"

Elena and Juanito had dropped their bundles on the ground to rest. Crispín approached Elena.

"Excuse me, ma'am. Tell me the number of your house and give me the key."

Crispín threw the bundles over his shoulder and walked off.

"Who is he, Papa?" asked Esperanza.

"He's one of the Madero council of two years ago. One of the gang," answered Don Juan, with a grimace of resignation and dislike.

"Well, I think he's a good man!"

Don Juan could not reply. His legs gave way and Esperanza had to hold him up until she could seat him on the curb.

Elena, with the baby on one arm and Juanito behind her, came up to help. The clock in a church tower slowly struck ten. They waited for Don Juan to rest. Only his heavy breathing broke the silence of the empty street. At the quarter hour Don Juan was still unable to move. At the half he seemed to be better, but he was breathing so easily that they all thought it would be a pity to disturb him. At eleven Don Juan got to his feet unaided, but at his first step he felt something rising in his throat. He could not breathe or even speak. He thought he was dying.

"A little longer . . . a little longer," he groaned. He sat down again.

Crispín found them in the same place.

"Just what I thought! How could he walk, much less get to the house? It's a hell of a way from here! Come, Don Juan, up you go!"

Don Juan objected in vain. Crispín picked him up in his strong arms and swung him over his back.

"Don Juan is fat, but it's all air. The bags were heavier."

They finally made it to the hut. Crispín wiped his face with a huge red bandana.

"The caciques!" he resumed. "Damn them! If there weren't any hell God should create one just for them! I got out of jail yesterday. They tied me up and kept me there for four months! Damned bandits! And only because I called them by their right names and said they made their money robbing widows, orphans, and defenseless people. Thieves in dress clothes! They're afraid of Villa and Zapata, but Villa and Zapata could take lessons from them! And just because Señor Rodríguez had the courage to tell them what they are they took him out and shot him! Bandits! Murderers!"

Esperanza fell fainting on a straw pallet. No one noticed.

"God's will be done! It's the will of God! *Dios te salve, María, llena de gracia!*" prayed Don Juan, crossing himself and counting the beads of his rosary.

But Crispín refused to stop until he had talked the bitterness out of his heart.

"Don't believe what that man says," said Don Juan, when Crispín had left. "It's all lies and slander! That's the way the members of the gang are!"

Esperanza was still unconscious. Juanito stood motionless, somber, and there was something frightening in his eyes, young as he was. Elena felt a lump in her throat.

They heard something that sounded like a groan, but is was only the wind making the door creak.

CHAPTER VI

"We're going for a walk today, Juanito," said Esperanza, as the two were returning to *La Carolina* after lunch. "I want you to take me to the country. I need some fresh air."

At four she led Juanito out to the edge of town. She was nervous and restless. After some apparently aimless wandering they found themselves at the cemetery gate. Esperanza's face was flushed. She looked about fearfully.

"You must be tired, Juanito," she said. "Sit here for a while. I want to walk by myself."

Slowly she made her way to the rear of the cemetery and scanned the furrows of the field. She saw the cross of rude sticks and hung upon it a small wreath which she took from her blouse.

Esperanza's eyes were burning when she returned to Juanito. She tried to hide her tears and pretended to watch the multicolored clouds sailing by overhead and to gaze at a distant village hazy in bluish smoke.

Juanito understood.

A sudden shadow darkened the field, as an immense flock of blackbirds passed whirring above them.

"Those who are coming will be as thick as that, Esperanza! The Revolution is coming!"

"Yes, it's time! I'll be glad!"

"Me too!" said Juanito, stamping his foot.

They walked home in silence.

CHAPTER VII

Lent had been a very bad season at *La Carolina*. Its proximity to the new building that Del Llanos Bros., Inc., were putting up kept it constantly immersed in a sea of dirt and dust, and its customers went elsewhere to trade.

The day Esperanza and Juanito were hired—almost out of charity, as the proprietors said—their single and unending task was to rid the counters and show cases of the dust blown in by the wild March wind from the new building. A few clerks talked together in low voices. Others sneezed. Everybody cursed the plasterers. Even ill humor, however, ends by becoming a bore, and finally the chief clerk folded his arms and spoke his mind.

"This new building of the Del Llanos is going to be the finest in the city. They originally planned to spend two hundred and fifty thousand on it, but it has already cost them more than three hundred thousand. It will cost half a million! It looks as if the Del Llanos have got too much money and are investing it in real estate for fear of the Revolution. Just look at it! The façade is of Guanajuato stone, a beautiful mottled green. And they're going in for real mosaic! The doors and windows were made by hand and must have cost a pretty penny. Anyone can see they've got too much! Over the main entrance they've carved an inscription to Mercury, the god of commerce, and his statue was done by an Italian sculptor. Why, it alone cost over a thousand pesos! On the ground floor, behind the shops, they're going to build living quarters. And what shops! They'll put us all out of business. Stocks of iron, copper, brass, fine and common lumber, French and native wines, corn, beans, grain—in short, everything, in the American style. They'll break us! And on the upper floor, offices and rooms for the employees, with inlaid floors. And some of the rooms, such as the private office of Don Ignacio, will be done in stucco. I've seen the plans. They'll ruin us, I tell you!"

The clerks listened open-mouthed. Juanito and Esperanza went back to their task of wiping off the dust that blew in ceaselessly.

Before seven the next morning, Esperanza and Juanito, on their way to work at *La Carolina,* stopped to look at the famous new building of the Del Llanos. Swarms of men were clambering like ants over the wooden scaffolding, the carved stone balustrades, the unfinished columns of the façade, and the steel frame of the domed roof which looked like a colossal spider web. Men, white with lime, their trousers rolled up to their copper thighs, were running up and down ladders. Others were laying bricks. Cranes groaned and creaked and hoisted great blocks of stone into the air.

Esperanza and Juanito watched the work, fascinated, until the clock struck seven. Neither of them spoke.

CHAPTER VIII

Elena was surprised by a visitor.

"I am the president of the Conference of St. Vincent de Paul. I understand that you have a very sick person here and I've come to bring help. Who is your doctor? You haven't got one? Good. Ours will take charge."

The neighborhood was interested. Word went round among the old women that the Divine Host was coming. At dusk the gray silhouette of the physician appeared, using his rolled umbrella as a walking stick. The women in the doorways, their babies clinging to their backs, stood up respectfully. Some ran to get paper, others ink or a chair, while the rest crowded into the room where Don Juan lay suffocating. An altar was improvised on a table, complete with brass crucifix, two wax candles, and many flowers.

The street lamps were lighted and gave off a feeble reddish glow on alternate corners. From the floor rose the smell of moist earth, roses of Castile and mallow, newly strewn against the coming of the Host.

The doctor arrived.

As the women moved about, their shawls and blankets clung to their skinny legs, flat breasts, and swollen bellies. Naked children, burned by the sun, rose from the dung hills with their hair full of chaff, wide-eyed.

"It's the doctor!" they said, and lost themselves

again in the earth. Dogs pricked up their ears and growled at him under their breath.

Over the door of the sick man's house an old curtain was hung, a sign that the Host was expected.

For two months Don Juan had not been able to sleep without having his head propped up with pillows, but that night he slept very well. He could hardly speak, but he said that he felt much better, thank God! And would they please put out the lights and go to bed? He wanted to sleep in comfort for one night, at least.

Elena consented, but after Esperanza and Juanito had gone to sleep, she arose in great anxiety, lit a candle, and approached Don Juan's bed on tiptoe.

Don Juan's life had flickered out quietly like a small flame.

Everyone got up.

By two in the morning the wax candle had burned out, but a beautiful moon was shining and a stream of moonlight poured over Don Juan's body for many minutes.

CHAPTER IX

"It seems more like September than April," observed one of the clerks at *La Carolina,* putting out his hand to catch the raindrops.

The noisy stream running in the gutter drowned out the ceaseless dripping of the rain. The light from the shop door made luminous patches on the black pond in the middle of the street which, stirred up by the current, broke into streaks of silver.

"Times are bad," complained the proprietor. "That damned building of the Del Llanos is ruining us. The construction is finished, but the rainy season has begun four months ahead of time and everyone has left town. It's hell!"

"The Del Llanos have all the luck," said a clerk. "Do you know how much they made out of that bankruptcy of the Olivares in San Luis Potosí? Well, the Olivares went broke for a hundred thousand, but Don Ignacio was smart and took their imported goods, so now at the present rate of exchange he's selling them for silver in Mexico City at a profit of a hundred and fifty per cent! He stands to make a cool hundred thousand out of it if he sells everything."

The proprietor bit his lips without answering.

Not a customer had come in for half an hour. The silent clerks, elbows on counters, listened to the monotonous whisper of the rain and the muffled strokes of eight.

Esperanza smoothed the fur of the spotted gray cat lying on the counter. The animal stretched, arched its back, and put out its claws. It lifted its head and its emerald eyes shone for a moment. Then it flattened its body, which was narrow at the neck and wide at the hips, dropped its head between its shoulders, and curled up again. Esperanza smothered a sigh.

"What do you know about the deal he made for the model village?" someone asked.

"Yes, yes, I know," the proprietor answered in a low voice, nudging the speaker and motioning toward Esperanza and Juanito. "They sold the place for a hundred thousand. And do you know how much it cost them? Well, it cost them ten thousand pesos, *ten thousand,* and at that I've put the figure too high. Why, the merchandise alone that they took from *La Sultana* more than paid for the construction. Sharks! Don Juan didn't even know what his stock was worth."

"Business is business," observed the proprietor dryly.

As sometimes happens with dying people, Esperanza's and Juanito's ears had become very acute.

Villegas, soaked to the skin, his shoes slopping over, burst into *La Carolina.*

"Gentlemen, a bit of news! The bandits are within five leagues of town! The Del Llanos are packing their trunks and are leaving immediately on a special train. I'm risking everything by staying here to look after the firm. Everything!"

The clerks stared at one another with bloodless faces and their knees trembled under them.

The proprietor sent them home.

The rain was coming down harder than ever. Juanito turned up the collar of his cotton coat. Esperanza rolled up her black calico dress, wound a shawl about her head, and the two, hugging themselves tightly, set out running through the dark deserted streets and the driving rain.

"Children, you're soaked!" cried Elena.

"Don't worry, Mama. Give us something to eat and we'll go straight to bed," said Esperanza, shivering.

Elena bowed her head. The pantry had been empty since noon and the pawnbroker had refused to lend her any more money.

"Don't cry, Mamacita! Tomorrow I'll ask for a two weeks' advance," said Esperanza. "Why didn't you tell me before?"

"I'm not hungry," said Juanito somberly.

"Neither am I," said Esperanza.

They spread their clothes on a broken couch, wrapped themselves up in the ragged blankets, and slept soundly till morning.

Juanito and Esperanza dashed out of *La Carolina,* which had hastily closed its doors, but they could hardly take a step. People were running and stumbling over each other.

"They're here! They're here!"

Doors banged noisily and the streets were suddenly empty.

First, a distant shot; then another, nearer, sharper, echoing like the explosion of a rocket. Then shots in all directions. Round a corner galloped a body of horsemen, their carbines raised. Hoofs struck sparks from the paving stones. Bullets passed whining.

Then the street was full of horsemen, their weather-beaten faces the color of earth, with eyes of wild beasts, in great straw sombreros covered with pictures of saints. Shooting in the air, they passed near where Juanito and Esperanza were standing, without seeing them.

Next came an avalanche of people, followed by a body of troops. Thousands of hands pointed to the doors of *La Carolina.* A soldier put his rifle to the lock and blew it off. The doors were opened with shouts and howls of joy. The people surged in and the looting began: cases of wine, cakes of brown sugar, sacks of corn and beans, mountains of cheese and canned goods.

Juanito watched. Esperanza shut her eyes tightly, as if expecting a bullet in her heart at any moment. Juanito gave a start.

"Esperanza, stay where you are and wait for me." Esperanza opened her eyes, uncomprehendingly. Juanito ran into *La Carolina* with the mob. A few seconds later he reappeared, painfully dragging a can of oil.

"Esperanza, come help me!"

Stunned, the girl was unable to move.

"Give me a hand! Look what I've got!"

Juanito motioned desperately with his eyes toward the huge edifice of the Del Llanos across the street.

Esperanza understood and ran to help him.

Juanito tried to open the tin with the edge of a stone, but the metal was tough and he could only dent it. He tore his hair with impatience. He tried again, and again failed. He turned his eyes in all directions.

"Here!" said Esperanza, taking a heavy pin from her hair.

Juanito punched a hole and then another. They sprinkled oil on the polished and freshly varnished door. The wood burned brightly. When the fire had eaten through the door they threw the can of oil inside and after it a blazing stick.

They heard an explosion and black smoke was soon pouring from the doors and windows. Then came the flames, licking the walls. Finally, from the top floor spirals of smoke rolled up to the clouds. The house of Del Llano Bros., Inc., burned very well.

Esperanza and Juanito did not hear the crack of the mausers, or the hoarse bark of the 30-30's, or the galloping of the horses. Entranced, hand in hand, their hearts beating wildly, they watched the flames mount to the purple sky.